THE REFERENCE SHELF *(Continued)*

THE REFERENCE SHELF

Vol. 31   No. 1

THE TWO GERMANIES

Edited by
GRANT S. McCLELLAN
Staff Member, Foreign Policy Association

THE H. W. WILSON COMPANY
NEW YORK   1959

19619

PREFACE

The status of Germany—now divided into two parts—remains after almost a decade and a half following World War II the most critical East-West problem in Europe.

Has Germany, at least West Germany, turned over a new leaf from the nation's autocratic past, not to mention the excesses of the Hitlerian dictatorship? Have the weaknesses of the inter-war democratic Weimar republic been overcome? And what of East Germany, now under Communist control? Is there a fair prospect that the two Germanies of today can be reunited in freedom? Or will the Communist-controlled portion of Germany prove to be a permanent feature of the European landscape?

A host of other problems are also involved today in any consideration of Germany—divided or not: the fate of the many thousands of refugees fleeing yearly into West Germany from the East; the role Germany will play in the movement for European integration; and what policies a rearmed Germany, unified or not, will pursue in the cold war.

American foreign policy today is deeply concerned about Germany as it has been ever since the war. If the cold war has seemed in the recent past to turn away from the European theater to a competitive economic cold war in the underdeveloped world of the Middle East and South Asia, it may now be on the verge of returning to Europe for still another round. Whether it will be an economic, political, or military contest (or a combination of all three), it will almost certainly center on Germany.

If East Germany has lagged behind the Western Federal Republic in economic recovery, there are now signs that it also is an economy of significance to the Communist orbit. East Germany's borders on the west lie only about three hundred miles from the English channel, obviously a fact of great strategic advantage to the Communist world.

Berlin, with its division between the Eastern and Western powers, lies one hundred miles within the Soviet zone of Germany, that is, the German Democratic Republic. In late November 1958, the Soviet Government in Moscow chose the status of this city as the occasion for its latest move in the East-West contest. Soviet Premier Nikita Khrushchev called on West Germany and the Western Big Three—France, Britain, and the United States—to renounce their positions in Berlin. He pledged that the city would become a "free city" and that West Berlin would be permitted to retain its free economy. With this move, the Western world began to gird itself for a new struggle with the Communist orbit in Europe.

This situation thus was far different from that of the early postwar period when European economic reconstruction was barely under way. It was different, too, from the days of the Berlin blockade which occasioned the "airlift" to rescue West Berlin in 1948-1949. Today, after a dramatic recovery, West Germany has become the Continent's foremost economic power. It is on the threshold of becoming West Europe's most powerful military nation. It is, at the same time, now closely integrated in various economic undertakings with other West European countries. And it is a full-fledged member of the North Atlantic Treaty Organization (NATO), the core alliance of Western defense.

Europe and the world have changed in revolutionary ways from the days at the end of the war with the rise of two superpowers outside Europe—the United States and Russia—and the development of new weapons of warfare which make any resort to military decision virtually a mutual suicide pact. In such a situation some of the old fears about Germany which haunted Europe, East and West, from the latter part of the nineteenth century until World War II have disappeared, if they have not been wholly forgotten. Since World War II one of the most striking facts about Europe's interstate relations has been the genuine *rapprochement* between the two long-time antagonists France and Germany.

In this situation the new Soviet proposals on Berlin or any attempt by the Russians to force a settlement for the whole of Germany is bound to mark a great divide in the cold war era.

That Germany may be a cause of war—this time not initiated by the nation which itself undertook war in Europe in 1914 and 1939—cannot be ruled out, however. Hence the articles in this compilation deal with some of the world's most critical issues. The further readings in the bibliography are especially recommended, since the problems discussed here are only raised and cannot be fully explored.

The editor wishes to thank the various authors, publishers, and organizations that have granted permission for the use of materials included in this book.

GRANT S. MCCLELLAN

February 1959

CONTENTS

THE TWO GERMANIES

Map showing the two Germanies which evolved from Western and Soviet postwar occupation zones. From New York *Times*. p E5. November 30, 1958. Reproduced by permission.

I. PERSPECTIVE ON GERMANY

EDITOR'S INTRODUCTION

The two Germanies of today can be properly viewed only against the background of the former unified nation. Not that Germany of pre-World War II was a nation with a long history of unity. It was, with Italy, one of the last European countries which we now identify as distinct nations to achieve unification. Historians debate the problem whether this was not in part the cause of the aggressive nature of the German national state under Bismarck, the Kaiser, and later Hitler. Regardless of this debate, however important, we know that Germany has in fact been a problem to Europe and to the West generally for several generations.

Some of the broader fundamental issues involved in Germany's past are dealt with in this opening section. First a historian of nationalism, Hans Kohn, briefly sketches the present status of the two Germanies. Theodor Heuss, now president of the Federal Republic of Germany and a former opponent of the Hitler regime, comments on the German character in the next article. No subject is perhaps more touchy, less subject to scientific analysis, whether the author deals with Germans or other nationalities. Of most concern here, however, is his forthright approach to his subject and the fact that he does not evade the problems of Germany's recent past. In the article by James B. Conant, former United States Ambassador to West Germany, a noted American also takes a look at Germany today in light of the period dominated by the Hitler dictatorship. He is optimistic that the West Germans have taken a new turn and welcomes them as partners in the Western alliance.

Last, a former German newspaper man, now a history teacher in the United States, discusses the first days of the Hitler regime which foreshadowed the excesses by which the Nazi dictatorship brought terror to Germany and later world war. He, too, is optimistic about Germany's future, though less so than some other authors in this compilation.

A NEW ERA FOR THE GERMAN PEOPLE? [1]

The year 1945 marked the greatest crisis in modern German history. It was not only the "thousand-year Reich" of the National Socialist regime which ended in utter collapse after only twelve years of existence. Prussia, which had largely determined German history for the past two hundred years, and the German Reich created by the Prussian, Otto von Bismarck, also collapsed.

Of Prussia no trace remained. The very name disappeared from the map. The Prussian ruling class, which had formed the core of the country's armed forces and bureaucracy, both long renowned for their efficiency, was dispossessed and dispersed. A chapter of German history—and because of Germany's power in the center of Europe, also of European history—had come to an end in 1945.

What most Europeans remembered were three recent fateful events—1914, the outbreak of the first great European war of the present century; 1933, the rise to power of Hitler; 1939, the year Hitler unleashed World War II. Thus Europe understandably wondered and worried what the future of Germany would be and what it would hold in store for the rest of the Continent. The Germans, however, were much too dazed in 1945 to ask themselves such questions. As in 1918, they were stunned by the Allied victory, which came after Germany had gloried in great military success.

But this time the situation was very different from that in 1918. The whole of Germany was occupied by foreign troops; the German cities lay in rubble; there was no German government in existence. Moreover, about 10 million German-speaking people expelled from Poland, Czechoslovakia and other Eastern and Central European countries poured into West Germany.

[1] From "West Germany: New Era for German People," by Hans Kohn, professor of history at the City College of New York. (Headline Series no 131) Foreign Policy Association. New York. September-October 1958. p3-16. Reprinted by permission.

These refugees represented a heavy drain on the resources of a half-starving population in a land where transportation was disrupted and normal economic life had come to a standstill.

The leaders of the three victorious allies—the United States, Britain and the U.S.S.R.—met at Potsdam near Berlin. According to the Potsdam agreement of August 2, 1945, eastern Germany was to be separated from Germany. A small part of it was to be administered by the U.S.S.R., which received the northern half of East Prussia with the important city of Königsberg, renamed Kaliningrad. By far the greater part was taken over by Poland. The Poles acquired all the lands east of the Oder and Neisse rivers, lands which the Poles regarded for historical reasons as their "recovered" territory.

The rest of Germany was divided into four occupation zones. The most populous one in northwestern Germany was allotted to the British; the U.S.S.R. and the United States occupied zones of approximately equal populations, the former in middle Germany, the latter in the southwest. The French were assigned a relatively small territory along the middle Rhine, including the Saar region. The former German capital of Berlin was occupied and administered jointly by all four powers. On all sides, however, Berlin was surrounded by Soviet-occupied territory.

Two Germanies

The hope of continuing cooperation among the victorious Allies soon disappeared, but at Potsdam the confidence in Communist good will had been so great that no provision was made for free access to Berlin for the Western Allies. [See "East-West Agreements," Section IV.—Ed.] In 1946 the Western Allies had no united policy against the Communist threat, nor did they cooperate among themselves. Their occupation zones were tightly insulated from each other. Although the Potsdam agreement regarded Germany under the four-power occupation as an economic unit, it was never treated as such, and each occupying power followed its own economic policy. Other points agreed upon in Potsdam were the trial of the Nazi war criminals and the denazification and democratization of German economic and political life. Only the first of these points, however, was carried out in November 1945 by all the powers acting in accord through the International Military Tribunal convened at Nuremberg, the once celebrated center of Nazi party manifestations. Otherwise, each occupying power followed its own distinct policy with regard to denazification and democratization.

Only after 1947 did the Western Allies, who had been eager to disarm and to return to a policy of normal peace, recognize the nature of Communist aggression. The widening breach between the democracies and the U.S.S.R. brought two results for Germany—closer cooperation among the Western Allies on the one hand, and a more stringent separation between the zones occupied by them, known as West Germany, and the Soviet-occupied zone, now generally called East Germany, on the other. These new designations were not merely geographic terms. The two parts of Germany became more and more disparate, socially and culturally. In West Germany democratic forms of life were introduced according to Western tradition. In East Germany, with its capital in Pankow [Northeast Berlin], the Russians imposed the social and cultural pattern of communism. Only Berlin remained as a point of continuing contact in which the two worlds—of democracy and communism—and the two Germanies met. From the Western point of view, West Berlin was a showcase of liberty in the midst of a Communist-oriented and Easternized society.

The Emergence of West Germany

Generally, from 1946 on, the Western Allies, in their zones, began to introduce democratic self-government based on free elections. They started from the grass roots with local and regional councils. Germany was divided into provinces, called *Länder,* each administered by its own cabinet of ministers. In 1948 the three Western occupation zones were merged and incorporated into the European Recovery Program, launched that year by the United States under the name of the Marshall Plan.

The most important decisions made by the foreign ministers of the Western countries in February 1948 was to call for a democratically-elected German constituent assembly, named the Parliamentary Council. Of real significance for the future of Germany was the Allied program that demanded a constitution which would "enable the Germans to play their part in bringing to an end the present division of Germany not by the reconstitution of a centralized *Reich* but by means of a federal form of government which adequately protects the rights of the respective states, and which at the same time provides for adequate central authority and which guarantees the rights and freedom of the individual."

After lengthy negotiations a German constitution, called the Basic Law, drafted in conformity with these expressed directives was adopted by the German Parliamentary Council on May 8, 1949, and went into force on May 23. The German Federal Republic was proclaimed on that day, and the first general election under the new constitution was held on August 14.

The new state was neither independent nor sovereign. Its foreign policy and many of its economic policies remained under the control of the Allies. The principal change was that Allied military governors were replaced by Allied high commissioners. John J. McCloy, now chairman of the Chase Manhattan Bank, became the first American high commissioner, replacing General Lucius D. Clay, the last American military governor. In spite of this continuation of the occupation the Western Allies regarded the Germans as "partners in an enterprise of mutual concern." They declared that "a restored and democratic Germany should be fully integrated, economically and politically, in a united Europe capable of resisting the threat of Communist imperialism." In the light of this statement it is understandable that the Soviet Union disapproved of the West's policy.

The determination of the Western Allies to see their zones integrated into a democratic Europe was countered by Russia's equally strong determination to keep its own zone a part of Communist Europe. A propaganda campaign was launched by the Communists to make West Germany appear as a forward bastion of the West preparing a new "Hitlerite" aggression against the Soviet Union. That the Hitlerite aggression in 1939 was directed against Poland and the West with Soviet support and encouragement was conveniently overlooked by the Kremlin. . . .

A Divided Country

The German Federal Republic, however, did not include the Soviet occupied zone and the city of Berlin. Nor had the fate of the Saar territory been decided in 1955. Thus Germany (outside the territories which had become for all practical purposes part of Poland and of the U.S.S.R.) consisted in 1955 of four different political entities.

AREA AND POPULATION IN DIVIDED GERMANY IN 1955

	Area (in sq. miles)	1955 Estimate of Population
German Federal Republic ..	94,733	49,696,000
Saar Territory	991	980,000
German Democratic Republic	41,380	16,721,000
Berlin	341	3,350,000

The Russian occupation authorities established in their zone the German Democratic Republic under strict Communist control. Reliable information about conditions in East Germany was as difficult to obtain as in other Communist-controlled lands. Wilhelm Pieck, a veteran Communist, was elected president, and Otto Grotewohl, a former Social Democrat, who had joined the Communists and established with them the Communist-directed Socialist Unity party, became chancellor. In June 1953 the workers in the German Democratic Republic demonstrated and rioted against economic conditions. Their uprising was suppressed, but it led to some improvement in the pitiful situation of the workers. The uprising, like the one three years later in Hungary, clearly indicated the unpopularity of the Communist regime, which in both countries seemed to depend largely on Russian armed might. An even better indication of the situation in the Soviet-occupied zone is the continuous stream of Germans who migrate to West Germany and West Berlin in quest of better living conditions and of political freedom.

The city of Berlin forms neither part of the German Federal Republic nor of the German Democratic Republic. In its social and cultural life it is divided into two different parts—West Berlin, with an area of 189.7 square miles and a population of around 2.2 million, and a smaller Eastern part. The Soviet government has made several attempts to force the Western Allies to surrender West Berlin, which has developed into a remarkable outpost of democracy behind the Iron Curtain. The most important of these attempts occurred in 1948, when the Communists imposed a blockade on all land traffic between West Berlin and the free world. This blockade was maintained for over ten months, and during that period the inhabitants of West Berlin were supplied with the necessities of life by an Anglo-American airlift. [A new effort to change the status of West Berlin occurred in late 1958. See Section IV.—Ed.]

Saar Settlement

The coal-rich and highly industrialized Saar territory was occupied after the war by the French, who established there an autonomous German administration and united it with France in economic and monetary matters. In 1945 this seemed to most Saarlanders a favorable solution. With Germany's rapid economic recovery, however, the mood changed.

An attempt was made to preserve a "European" status for the Saar. In 1955 Chancellor Adenauer agreed with the French government that the territory should become the responsibility of the Western European Union, to which both France and West Germany belonged, and that the status of the Saar would again be taken up when a final peace treaty with Germany was concluded. In a plebiscite in October 1955, however, only one third of the Saar population voted for such a European solution. Two thirds of the voters, consisting mainly of German nationalists and Social Democrats, rejected this status. Thereupon the future of the Saar was settled through Franco-German negotiations which were successfully concluded in the autumn of 1956. On January 1, 1957, the Saar became politically an integral part, a *Land,* of the German Federal Republic, while remaining for three more years economically united with France. In return France received certain economic concessions from Germany. The happy solution of the thorny Saar problem, which had poisoned Franco-German relations after World War I, was an indication of the lessened nationalist temper in both France and West Germany and of the latter's changed attitude toward cooperation with its Western neighbors.

West Germany and Europe

Germany's partition, like that of Korea and Vietnam, is not a cause but a consequence and a symptom of the world-wide tension between democracy and communism. These three divided nations have not yet become members of the United Nations. But West Germany has been accepted as a member of all the specialized agencies of the United Nations [like] the International Labor Organization (ILO) [and] the Food and Agriculture Organization (FAO). . . .

More important, however, is West Germany's cooperation with the various agencies and organizations which since 1948 have laid the foundation of European integration. Germany was admitted as a full member of the Council of Europe in May 1951. In August 1952 the European Coal and Steel Community (ECSC) was created, marking the first step toward a supranational form of integration. Its members are Belgium, France, Germany, Italy, Luxembourg and the Netherlands. Among these six nations Germany was economically the most powerful by 1958.

On January 1, 1958, two new economic communities, uniting the six European nations, came into existence—the European Economic Community, which is to become in the course of the next twelve years a common market, and the European Atomic Energy Community. On March 21, 1958, the deliberative body of the three economic communities met for the first time in Strasbourg, France, as a European Parliamentary Assembly. Such close cooperation between Germany and the rest of Western Europe would have been unthinkable before 1945.

GERMAN CHARACTER [2]

History recognizes a few cases of nations which manifest themselves as intellectual and spiritual unities. But few who really know America, for example, are satisfied with attempts to portray a definitive type of "the American," in spite of the . . . consistent rhythm that may be observed in that country as the result of 450 years of opening up a continent, settling it, and developing it at a tremendous pace. The situation is inevitably the same for the Germans. . . .

History . . . denied the Germans the opportunity to shape their own political destiny democratically. This was not due to any basic trait in the "German nature." The Germans, too, "fought for freedom"—in the peasant wars of the Reformation and in the civic uprisings of 1848, to name the most prominent examples. But theirs was a history of defeats which did not lend themselves to legends of glory. After the military collapse of 1918 and the abdication of all the dynastic sovereigns, a democratic constitution was set up as the sole possible basis for a legitimate government. But this democracy was not a prize won in hard struggle; it was simply seized upon in desperation. . . .

It is time to discontinue the practice of considering individuals as necessarily representative of national character. The Germans would love to say simply: "Our Goethe!" But they might hear, from a good many quarters, a responding echo: "Your Hitler!"

We cannot bow that man Hitler out of the German consciousness. We must not even want to. For his memory remains for the Germans a warning of the excesses which follow if amorality, immorality, becomes established as the law of the land. Only it is unfair to proclaim him an exponent of the German character. In the technique of power Hitler was a disciple of Mussolini, as Mussolini was a follower of Lenin. . . . Hitler, however, with the abominable consistency of the half-educated, chose as his guiding principle a form of biological naturalism—the annihilation of the Jew. . . .

[2] From "German Character and History," by Theodor Heuss, president of the Federal Republic of Germany. Translated by Richard and Clara Winston. Published in a supplement, "Perspective of Germany," in *Atlantic Monthly*. 200: 103-9. March 1957. Reprinted by permission of Intercultural Publications, Inc.

The Germans are still in the stage of evolving their political life. Because in the past century and a half they have witnessed both at home and abroad—or endured—such varied conditions of power and have been offered such heterogeneous political and social ideologies, they have been inclined to overrate the importance of theory. . . .

Foreigners tend to see such dogmatism as peculiarly German in contrast to Latin, Anglo-Saxon, and Slavic attitudes. Even Germans take this view—some irritably maintaining that doctrinairism expresses the humorlessness of underlings, others pridefully reminding us that, after all, Germany is a land where "order reigns"—even in party politics. This widely credited legend of the German sense of order or "talent for organization" reflects the simple fact that the average German is hard-working because traditionally he had to be; there has been no other way for him to earn his living in a country so restricted in area. And yet, the historical complexities of German public life show what an empty slogan this is. Organizational perfectionism in matters of detail may sometimes have smothered creative initiative. But over-organization seems often to accompany deep changes in social structure.

While, on the one hand, the German is supposed to be a pedant obsessed with accuracy, on the other hand he is pictured as a wildly imaginative romantic, in both philosophy and politics, allegedly more given to shattering patterns than to shaping or consolidating them. Naturally such a type does exist among the Germans (as, incidentally, from Germany's point of view, both types occur in foreign nations). . . .

The Germans of this generation labor under a burden of ill fate: proclaiming that they were the bringers of salvation, they have actually brought a curse upon the world. In the enormities that were committed, the "demonism" of power-madness was combined with personal brutality and the pedantry of the totalitarian [under the Hitlerian regime]. They have no right to excuse themselves by crying their own woes or pointing to the injustice of "others." But it is permissible to recall that worldwide condemnation, such as the Germans have now brought upon themselves, was applied 150 years ago to the French people. They were then charged with being eternal trouble-makers. And, historically, the "imperialism" of the Spaniards, the British, the French, the Russians, and even the Swedes was actually of a greater order of magnitude, in terms of territory. Here again, then, we are not dealing with a peculiar feature of the German constitution. Rather, such excesses are judged more harshly today because the extension of international law and the codification of civil liberties have rendered man's conscience more sensitive.

There remains the difficult question of whether a peculiar faculty for abstraction inheres in the German character as such, expressed in realms other than political and social history. To my mind, romanticism is no evidence for it. . . . Romanticism as an attitude and profession of faith was born in England. Compared to Byron and Shelley, almost all the German roman-ticists (except such figures as E. T. A. Hoffmann and Clemens Brentano) were good sober citizens. . . .

But now we confront the peculiar dichotomy of the century from 1750 to 1850—these dates being intended merely as rough limits. It was the age of classical poetry, of the great [German] thinkers (Lessing, Kant, Schiller, Fichte, Hegel, Schelling, Schopenhauer), and of a tremendous wave of great music. . . .

Perhaps the German has a special talent for "ideological" thinking; perhaps he is peculiarly susceptible to its appeal. At times this gift may seem to surround him with a handsome aureole; at other times it produces general distrust, and he is seen as a decidedly equivocal fellow, whose intellectual and spiritual life cannot be plumbed. Some Germans are aware of the disadvantages of being so unpredictable—other peoples with a history full of vicissitudes are also familiar with this problem. When the German takes refuge in self-praise—sometimes a man-ifestation of a sense of weakness—he speaks of his "profundity."

Nowadays he has little time for such attitudes. He must try once more to get a grip on the world from which he was shut off for so long, and which was presented to him only in dis-torted fashion—just as his own image had changed in the eyes of the world: a fact he was naïvely astonished to learn. He has come to realize (except for those who like to cultivate a sense of grievance) that such misconceptions must be cleared up. . . .

A strange and still obscure process of psychological change is going forward in Germany. It remains to be seen whether and how new characteristic attitudes and a new intellectual style will develop. There are now communities and districts in Germany which contain up to 40 per cent of "new citizens" from territories long settled by Germans in the East and Southeast. In some cases friendships and mixed marriages are formed, in other cases discontents and hostilities arise because traditions are being upset. Even while spiritual and economic fusion is taking place in certain areas, we can also see all manner of efforts to preserve and cherish the values which are, especially for the rural and small-town populace, bound up with the native soil in which their forefathers rest. . . .

Such are some of the questions Germans have in mind when they look to the future, questions of a people's rebirth and destiny.

THE SPIRIT OF GERMANY [3]

The spirit of Germany today is the spirit of a people who have repudiated the tyranny and brutality of the Nazi rule.

Perhaps some, . . . still thinking in terms of 1945, may question this generalization. Let me therefore . . . present concrete evidence to support my contention that nazism is dead and buried. First let us remember how the leaders of present-day Germany suffered during the period of the Nazi rule. Chancellor Adenauer was removed from his office as mayor of Cologne in 1933 for his bold defiance of Hitler, banished from the city, and more than once arrested and threatened with execution; President Theodor Heuss, the author of a book warning against Hitler when the future dictator was building up a following, was forced to live in obscurity for the twelve years of Nazi rule. Leaders of political parties, the mayors of many

[3] From "The Federal Republic of Germany, Our New Ally," speech originally given as a Gideon D. Seymour Memorial Lecture at the University of Minnesota on February 24, 1957, by James B. Conant, former President of Harvard University, and former United States Ambassador to the West German government. University of Minnesota Press. Minneapolis. 1957. p 1-20. Reprinted by permission.

cities, the heads of the governments of the states, have been out-spoken critics of the Nazi methods and goals. Indeed, I could draw up a long list of men and women who speak for free Germany today and who are no hypocrites when they denounce the Nazi past, for they themselves were always in opposition— not a few at the risk of imprisonment, torture, and execution.

But are the views of these Germans popular? does the bulk of the population agree with their assessment of the past? a skeptic may well ask. My answer would be yes. Look at the results of the national elections in the Federal Republic in 1953 and the state elections since. No right radical party has obtained enough votes to win representation in either the national or the state assemblies. And, what is equally impressive, the out-spoken critics of the Nazi past have been repeatedly elected to national, state, and municipal posts. What Americans often fail to realize is the extent to which Hitler and his intimates completely discredited themselves by their actions during the last few years of the total war. The barbarous revenge which Hitler took after the attempt to destroy him by a bomb on July 20, 1944, his senseless last-ditch resistance in Berlin when the war was clearly lost, his repeated statements that he would bring all Germany down in ruins about him, his orders to flood the mines and destroy the industry (orders which were never carried out)—all these things are well known in Germany and have left their mark. So too have the revelations of the horrors of the concentration camps and the slaughter of the Jews. Therefore, speaking as a reporter of the German scene, I think it correct to state that the legend of Hitler and the Nazis has no hold whatsoever on the German people. If there should be another significant right radical movement in Germany, such a movement, I feel sure, will not employ the symbols of the Nazis or claim any connection with their history, their slogans, or their goals. I realize full well the dangers of proph-ecy, but this one statement I make as a prophet with complete assurance.

I have opened my talk today about our new ally, our new NATO partner, with a consideration of the attitude of the Germans toward their past for one very simple reason. Mutual trust and understanding are essential for the functioning of an alliance. It is not easy to establish this relationship between two peoples who have twice fought each other bitterly within forty years. And the key to straight thinking by Americans about Germany is to be found in understanding how Germans themselves assess that terrible period when Hitler and his followers threatened the freedom of the world. In the official brochure describing the rebuilding of the city of Wurzburg, the mayor calls on his fellow citizens on each anniversary of the great air raid which nearly destroyed the city "to recall how brutal and degrading was the spirit which spread itself throughout our nation and among our people from 1933 to 1945." In another city heavily destroyed, the citizens erected a memorial on which stands the inscription "The dead admonish us—1933 to 1945." The significance of the date 1933, the date when Hitler came to power, is not lost on any German.

The first prerequisite to understanding our new NATO partner I have just considered. . . . Let me now turn to the second. This involves a bit of knowledge of modern geography as well as of modern history. . . . The map shows Germany divided and the city of Berlin isolated—an outpost of freedom, we often say. . . .

Let me now direct your attention to that portion of Germany which was once composed of the British, French, and American zones of occupation. The presence of Allied troops along the eastern boundaries of this area, like the presence of the troops in free Berlin, has been the deterrent to Soviet expansion. At least that is my firm belief and a belief that is shared by the great majority of Germans. Officially the Allied forces were occupation forces until in May 1955 the Federal Republic of Germany became sovereign. But they have been regarded as defenders, not occupiers, ever since the days of the Korean War and the resulting alarm in Europe as to the possibilities of military invasion from the east. As part of the NATO forces they have been and still are protecting not only the Federal Republic of Germany but the freedom of the West. But they no longer stand alone, for a German army is coming into being. . . . The Federal Republic of Germany is in fact as well as in principle our military ally and an ally with increasing strength.

The reaction here in the United States toward German rearmament seems to be a bit ambivalent. . . . On the one hand, I have heard some Americans complain because the process had been too slow, while others are worried because it is occurring at all! The latter, perhaps, are too inclined to speak of German militarism as if the two words, German and militarism, were inseparably connected; and remembering what happened in the 1920's and 1930's, they are apprehensive about the future. The first and larger group of Americans, who are impatient at the delay in bringing German soldiers to the support of the other NATO troops, fails to realize that Germany was completely demilitarized in the first years of occupation and that the building of a military establishment from scratch is no simple undertaking.

To be sure, the Federal Republic has gone about this business of creating an armed force with prudence and caution—a caution which I believe to be justified. But this attitude has undoubtedly caused delays. For example, the leaders of all the political parties have been anxious to create a constitutional basis for the armed forces which would make impossible a repetition of what has occurred in German history when the soldiers have determined internal and external policies. They wished to avoid the creation of a state within a state, or rather, they wished to be as certain as they could that the spirit of the new German army was in accord with the democratic mood of Germany today. Therefore, new laws were carefully drafted and, in addition, a committee of prominent citizens of different political persuasions was set up to review the records of all persons nominated by the defense department for the positions of colonel or higher; this committee had complete veto on such appointments and used it in more than one instance. As a result, all parties seem satisfied that the officer corps will be free from any taint of nazism and will be dedicated to the defense of a democratic Germany in alliance with other NATO nations. . . .

At this point I must insert a few words about German recovery. . . . Economics cannot be separated from politics, so let me remind you of what happened in the Western zones of occupation between the war's end and 1955 when the Federal Republic became sovereign. The currency reform of 1948 was the first essential for German recovery; closely related was the creation of a government with a banking system that issued a stable currency. Indeed if anyone ever needed evidence as to the importance of sound money, the recent history of Germany provided the material. From the close of the war until the summer of 1948 very little progress was made in rebuilding the cities and industrial plants, trade was largely on a barter basis, the stores were almost empty. But as soon as the new currency was introduced into the three Western zones, conditions changed almost overnight: people began to work, trade to function— recovery began.

Shortly after the currency reform, the Western Allies assisted the Germans in their zones in creating a national government. In the summer of 1949 the first elections under the new constitution were held. When the lower house, the Bundestag, assembled, the machinery of parliamentary government started to function. Konrad Adenauer was elected chancellor. The economic policy of his government, the policy of Minister for Economics Professor Erhard, proved admirably suited for the tasks which lay ahead. Private initiative and competition were encouraged, socialization of industry was rejected, tax laws were passed which enabled industry to put back its profits into plant reconstruction. And it has been largely by plowing back profits that the industrial recovery has taken place. Of course the impetus given by American aid through the Marshall Plan was of the greatest importance, and that this is so is freely acknowledged by Germans in all walks of life. All told, the American taxpayer has contributed some three and a half billion dollars to the reconstruction of Germany. But I might note that no new aid has been given during the last five years except for the city of Berlin. . . .

To the factors I have mentioned should be added three others in explaining German recovery. First, the attitude of the labor leaders who during the critical years refrained from pushing demands for increased wages. Second, the *esprit de corps* of the technical staff and working forces in many factories which enabled these plants to start functioning again as soon as equipment could be put in order and raw materials obtained. Third, the well-known desire of the German people to work hard and effectively once a sound basis is at hand.

German material recovery is an amazing fact. The economic basis of our new ally is as solid as one could wish: the currency is strong, the gross national product rises strikingly with each passing year. What about the political stability? Anyone who remembers Germany of the Weimar Republic days is likely to raise this question. For the Weimar Republic did not function well, the political leaders of those days failed to make democracy work. To be sure, Hitler's success in the 1930's can be attributed very largely to the vast unemployment caused by the world-wide depression that started in 1929. But even before the depression hit Germany, parliamentary government was hardly a great success. . . .

The political history as well as the economic history of the Federal Republic of Germany is thus the story of the successful efforts of a free people. . . .

Let us take a quick glance at the conditions in the Soviet zone. . . . The regime carries the name "The German Democratic Republic," but what a travesty of democracy is actually in operation is evident from the way the Peoples' Chamber, the alleged legislative body, was elected. The procedure was a farce. The so-called Social Unity Party (in reality the Communist Party) controls everything within the zone, including the sham parties which bear names similar to the leading parties in the Federal Republic. The schools and universities have been remodeled to fit the Communist pattern. All publications must conform to the party line; the industries have been largely nationalized, agriculture reshaped to conform to the Communist ideology. With what little favor all this has been received by the population was made evident on June 17, 1953, when a spontaneous uprising occurred in East Berlin. Soviet troops and tanks had to be called for by the Communist officials, for their own East German police proved to be completely unreliable. The spirit of freedom which was symbolized in those days by the young men who threw stones at the Soviet tanks still burns strongly throughout the zone. Of

that I have not the slightest doubt. If free elections were held
in the Soviet-occupied territory tomorrow, the Communist regime
and its hangers-on would be repudiated by a vote of at least
9 to 1.

From what I have just said about the Soviet zone . . . it is
obvious that the uppermost political problem in Germany must
be the problem of how to achieve reunification. The position of
the French, the British, and the United States governments has
been repeatedly set forth by notes and at conferences with the
Soviets. We ask that an all-German government come into being
by a process of free elections throughout all Germany, including
of course the Soviet zone. Such a government would represent
the 17 million Germans now living under Soviet domination as
well as the 50 million in the Federal Republic. All the parties in
the Federal Fepublic have agreed with this proposal: all parties
agree that only a freely elected all-German government is competent to represent Germany in negotiating a peace treaty which
will settle the boundaries of the nation. The Soviets have repeatedly rejected this solution and in recent years have demanded
as a first step toward reunification consultations between representatives of their puppet regime, the so-called German Democratic Republic, and the Federal Republic. . . .

If we are to understand Germany today, we Americans must
get our ideas straight about the situation in the Soviet zone and
the way Germans think about it. When it comes to making
proposals about German reunification, I would suggest that all
individuals who discuss this matter keep in mind the distinction
between the phrase one hears repeatedly in free Germany "reunification in peace and freedom" and the signs in the Soviet
zone which proclaim "Germans around one table; the social
achievements of the German Democratic Republic must be pre-
served." The Soviets and their agents are ardent supporters of
reunification, but *not* reunification in freedom; what they look
forward to is a reunited Communist-controlled Germany. And
Americans are too prone, in my opinion, to wave aside the danger
of such a possibility. For some individuals who from time to
time have put forward proposals for reunification have failed, I
believe, to give sufficient consideration to preserving peace and

guaranteeing freedom. There is at present no basis for believing
that Soviet intentions have changed or that the danger from
Soviet ambition has diminished. Until there is some prospect of
a general settlement of the tensions of a divided world, it would
seem to me extremely perilous to leave a united Germany pro-
tected only by its own military forces, assuming for the sake of
argument the Soviets would agree to any such arrangement. The
withdrawal of American troops from Europe seems to me far too
high a price to pay for reunification; and I know many, many
Germans would agree with this conclusion. . . .

We are allied to the free people of Germany today in defense
of Europe. The only government entitled to speak for them, the
freely elected government of the Federal Republic, is by its own
declaration a provisional government since it has been elected by
only the inhabitants of what were once the American, British,
and French zones. While praising its accomplishments, . . . we
must hope for its eventual replacement by an all-German government freely elected by all the Germans. This is the paradox of
the present, a result of the tragic split of Germany today. As the
governments of the United States, Great Britain, and France have
repeatedly declared, there can be no hope of a lasting peace and
security in the world until German reunification is achieved—
until an all-German government is established in Berlin. When
that day comes, the history of the Federal Republic will have
been concluded. . . . I have attempted to give you as objective a
report as possible on our new ally. I trust my words may con-
tribute something toward a better understanding between the
German and the American people, for I am convinced the world's
hopes for peace and freedom depend to no small degree on the
success of our present cooperation.

THE HITLERIAN NIGHTMARE [4]

It was Wednesday, May 10, 1933. . . . Midnight was approaching. Thousands of students and Nazi functionaries were

[4] From "First Hundred Days of the Hitler Nightmare," article by Felix E.
Hirsch, former German newspaper editor, now professor of history at Trenton State
College, Trenton, N.J. New York *Times Magazine.* p 14-15+. May 11, 1958.
Reprinted by permission.

assembled on the Opera Square in the heart of Berlin, just a short distance from the university which had been founded by Wilhelm von Humboldt, Germany's greatest liberal thinker.

The crowd had gathered to watch the burning of twenty thousand books written by "decadent" authors. The public jeered when student leaders shouted their names and cited their "crimes." On the pyres landed the works of Albert Einstein and Sigmund Freud, Thomas and Heinrich Mann, Emil Ludwig and Erich Maria Remarque, Walther Rathenau and Stefan Zweig and, last but not least, Theodor Heuss, today West Germany's president.

As the flames were consuming their books, the "little doctor," Joseph Goebbels, the Minister of Propaganda, climbed the rostrum and started to talk in his usual vitriolic fashion. This bonfire, he said, was a great symbolic act. It demonstrated to the world that the intellectual foundations of the old order had been destroyed. The German folk soul could again express itself. Goebbels ended with the words of a humanist poet: "Oh century, it is a joy to live!"

The night of May 10, 1933, came as the culmination of a hundred days of horror, a hundred days that changed the face of Germany as no student of its history could ever have foreseen. It was as if a violent fever had gripped the nation. Cherished values and century-old traditions collapsed over-night. Who cared for established rights or the demands of common decency?

Each of those evil days was fraught with personal danger, human disappointment, political disaster. My friends and I who stayed on temporarily in our editorial positions at the *Berliner Tageblatt,* which had been Germany's greatest democratic newspaper, knew that we were fighting a losing battle, that the ideals in which we believed were doomed and that exile would eventually be our lot, if we should be able to get out at all.

The first shock had come on January 30, about noon. . . . I was thunder-struck when I read the news. President Paul von Hindenburg had appointed as Chancellor Adolf Hitler—the very man whom he had decisively defeated for the presidency in the elections of the preceding spring! Even worse, two of Hitler's lieutenants, Wilhelm Frick and Herman Goering, had taken over the ministries of the interior in the Reich and in Prussia! That meant that Goering had gained control of the Prussian police, the last strong bulwark of the democratic order. The Weimar Republic had been sold down the river.

That evening, the *Deutsche Allgemeine Zeitung,* a moderate newspaper, used the prophetic words: "It was comparatively easy to appoint Hitler, but it will be less easy to oust him from office." The same night, Goebbels organized a torchlight parade through the Wilhelmstrasse, the seat of the government. Tens of thousands of S. A. storm troopers, S. S. élite guards and *Stahlhelm* veterans marched and jubilantly saluted Hindenburg and Hitler. Anybody watching that parade realized that a new era was beginning.

In the evening of February 27, the phone rang at my home. On the other end was our news editor. In his usual calm way he said: "May I suggest you take a taxi and go to the Reichstag? The building is afire."

Arriving on the spot a quarter of an hour later, I found it impossible to pass through the police cordon and get close to the Parliament. Even my so-called police passport, which had always enabled me to cross through such lines, had lost its magic. No precise information could be obtained on the fire and its mysterious origin.

That night, the real reign of terror began. The government accused the Communists of having organized the fire and used this as a convenient excuse for drastic action. From then on, secret police and storm troopers raided the homes of political enemies, abducting them under the cover of night. For many of the victims, a long period of interrogations, cruel beatings and tortures began. To escape a similar fate, I changed my quarters every night in those critical weeks.

In the Reichstag elections of March 5 the Nazis received only 44 per cent of the popular vote; they still needed the German Nationalist party to obtain a clear majority. Nevertheless, they retained the initiative, since the opposition was divided and uncertain of its course. On March 23, the new Reichstag passed the Enabling Act which permitted Hitler to dispense with the most important articles of the Weimar constitution. His victory was complete. Now, step by step, he could carry through his program.

An anti-Semitic boycott was organized with brutal thorough-ness on April 1. It lasted only one day, but it indicated what fate would be meted out to the Jewish citizens of Germany eventually. The next measures were directed against the working class. Following a May Day celebration, the powerful trade unions were taken over by the Nazis. Finally, on the same day on which the books were burned, Hitler seized the headquarters of the Social Democratic party, once the backbone of the Weimar Republic. In just one hundred days he had made himself master of Germany. Twelve years of oppression were to follow.

How was it possible that a ruthless demagogue like Hitler could emerge and gain total control of his adopted country [Hitler was an Austrian by birth—Ed.] without ever obtaining a majority at the polls? No one cause explains this phenomenon adequately. A number of factors had to come together, before President von Hindenburg could be persuaded to entrust the reins of government to the "Austrian corporal," whom he despised.

Hitler's movement had gained its initial strength from his oratorical fight against the Versailles Treaty, especially its war-guilt clause. Many former army officers and students had been impressed by the legend he told of the "stab in the back," by which the Left-wing parties had allegedly prevented German victory in World War I.

Since early 1930, the world depression had been affecting the German economy more and more severely. Millions of workers and white collar people lost their jobs. While the government preached deflation as the major cure, Hitler promised the sky to the jobless.

Hitler's arguments were especially attractive to young people, university students and proletarians alike. Many of them were fed up with the cold realism of the old-style politicians and trade union leaders. Hitler offered these adolescents a "cause" around which to rally. Every week-end there were bar-room brawls or real street battles in some industrial cities with *Rot Front*, the Communist party fighters, or the *Reichsbanner*, the political army of the pro-Weimar parties. Young people who had nothing more constructive to do might actually think that they were defending their Fatherland on such occasions. Their feelings were confirmed by many nationalistic newspapers, which helped to poison public opinions by vicious partisanship.

To these psychological and social factors must be added the structural weaknesses of the Weimar Republic. They facilitated the emergence and indeed the victory of Hitler. The power of Parliament was pulverized by the competition of six or more major parties, none of whom ever acquired a clear-cut majority. This led to the formation of heterogeneous coalitions. Votes of no-confidence were frequent; governments changed constantly. Chancellor Bruening had to rule largely by emergency decrees signed by von Hindenburg.

This would have been a tolerable expedient if the chief of state had been a resourceful younger man, experienced in politics and of firm convictions. But the aged Field Marshal had none of these qualities. At the age of eighty-five, he could hardly be expected to handle much of the executive business. Three men had practically taken control of his affairs: his son Oskar, his Secretary of State, Otto Meisner, and his favorite, Franz von Papen, a past master of political intrigue whom he chose as Bruening's successor and who finally served as go-between with Hitler in the secret negotiations of January 1933.

The Reichswehr High Command was another factor behind the scenes. It was represented by General Kurt von Schleicher; smooth and unprincipled, he was not a strong chancellor in the brief interval between von Papen's downfall and Hitler's appointment. Lastly, there were Hindenburg's old Junker friends who trembled for their bankrupt estates and hoped that Hitler would save them from the "bolshevism" of the Republic. In the end, it was this combination of extraconstitutional forces which swayed the bewildered President. On his own, he would never have called Hitler to office.

No doubt, the major responsibility for the events of the spring of 1933 rests with von Hindenburg and his circle. But many of the democratic parliamentarians come in for their share of the guilt also. Weak, unimaginative, defeatist, they did little to prevent the catastrophe when there was still time.

During the year 1933 I had ample opportunity to study human nature as it unfolds under a dictatorship. It was fascinating to observe how different types behaved under the impact of a diabolic propaganda and all kinds of pressures and temptations. The old trade union members who had had their political education in the Social Democratic party, such as many of the printers in our publishing house, never wavered in their allegiance. They could not be lured by any dictatorship, brown or red. No wonder that workers like these were among the stoutest fighters in West Berlin's battle for freedom after World War II.

Equally uncompromising were some liberal democrats, the heirs of the traditions of 1848. Two names may suffice: Arnold Brecht and Theodor Heuss. Brecht, Prussia's brilliant spokesman in the Reichsrat, the upper legislative house representing the German states, dared to address Hitler publicly on the sanctity of the oath which the new Chancellor had sworn on January 30. Hitler left the room without reply and Brecht was dismissed a few days later.

Heuss had the tenacity to edit *Die Hilfe,* an old respected journal of opinion, as if there was no such thing as the Nazi dictatorship. The term *"Der Fuehrer"* was never used in its pages, nor was any concession made to the government propaganda line. The editor had the courage to open his columns to such inconvenient contributors as this writer. The idyll lasted until 1936 when Goebbels put an end to it, but Heuss emerged from the Third Reich with an untarnished reputation. . . .

Many younger scholars were eager to adjust their thinking to the whims of the new rulers, hoping for professorships and other tangible rewards for their "flexibility." But most of the old luminaries, with some painful exceptions, did not change their values or their friendships. . . .

Even more vigorous was the opposition of some old conservatives. They had not liked the Republic, but they detested the new masters. Among these upright conservatives were many Protestant clergymen. When, in the troubled days of 1933, I wanted to hear a ringing message on the rights of man, I would travel to the suburb Dahlem on a Sunday morning. Martin Niemoeller was preaching there to an ever-increasing flock with a fearlessness and a fervor that reminded his listeners of his name-sake Martin Luther. Imprisonment would later be his lot and that of many other courageous clergymen.

But most other groups were ready to get on the Nazi band-wagon with rather indecent haste. Cherished convictions were dropped overnight. The swastika was hoisted from balconies; the *Voelkische Beobachter,* Hitler's own paper, appeared on living room tables; soon memberships in some Nazi organization were secured.

There were many businessmen who felt that the new regime would be sympathetic to their interests and who were delighted about the wrecking of the trade unions. Many members of the professional class and of the higher civil service sensed that *Gleichschaltung* (political coordination) might benefit their careers. They were too intelligent not to recognize the excesses of the new regime, but they professed confidence that Hitler himself would eventually correct the mistakes of his lieutenants.

The small middle class had always been critical of the Weimar Republic and longed for the return of the "good old Prussian order." This social group contained also traditionally the greatest number of genuine anti-Semites who, of course, were pleased by the misfortunes of the Jews. Among the most fanatical adherents of the regime were some idealistic women who outdid themselves in adulation of Der Fuehrer.

Could history repeat itself and Germany come again under the spell of a maniac? The historian hesitates to make prediction, but perhaps he can derive a few insights from the past.

I see one reason for concern in the rapid changes of the German political temper as I observed them under the Weimar Republic. To give but one example that comes to memory: As I watched from a window of the Reichstag the tremendous demonstrations on the tenth anniversary of the Constitution (August 11, 1929), it would never have occurred to me that a landslide would bring 107 Nazi members into that same building only thirteen months later. Is a similar change of temper possible now? How deeply ingrained is the democratic idea in the country today? Is the miraculous economic prosperity, which may now have reached or passed its peak, the main source of its popularity, or have the Germans really learned a lesson in politics?

Despite such questions, the odds are against the rise of another Hitler. The horrors of the second World War, which the Germans experienced in their homes, have taught them what the defeat on foreign soil in the first World War failed to convey to them: that aggressive nationalism does not pay. There are some other promising signs. My fellow students at German universities in the early 1920's were in the vanguard of nazism. But, when I taught and lectured there in 1954-1955, many of my students turned out to be fervent adherents of European cooperation and international peace.

Generally speaking, public opinion in Western Germany today is more liberal, more world-minded, supranational organizations like Euratom and the Common Market are backed vigorously. No newspaper peddles the vicious nationalism that was the stock in trade of Hitler's and Hugenberg's papers twenty-five years ago.

The men who framed the Bonn Constitution, above all President Heuss and Chancellor Adenauer, make a concerted effort to prevent a repetition of the tragic errors which had doomed the first republic. The role of the president, for instance, has been limited mostly to symbolic functions. The executive is now clearly under the control of the chancellor. The Bundestag (Federal Diet) cannot dislodge him, unless a majority has agreed on the formation of another cabinet. This has given Adenauer's regime the stability for which Weimar statesmen had striven in vain.

Every election since 1949 has increased the trend toward a system of few parties. Adenauer's Christian Democratic Union gained in 1953 and even more convincingly in 1957 a clear-cut majority in the Parliament such as the old Reichstag never knew. These victories may be largely attributed to Adenauer's statesmanship and personality, but the octogenarian Chancellor has seen to it that the CDU sent a lot of younger talent to the Bundestag. When he and Heuss step down from their positions, their successors may be chosen from a remarkable reservoir of able and dedicated men. This is a great reassurance, when we remember the dearth of true leadership in the Weimar Republic. Also there is a loyal opposition in Bonn today, represented by Social Democrats and Free Democrats. They could be trusted to uphold civil liberties just as faithfully as the CDU does.

At this point, the Bonn Republic is not bothered by extremist movements. The right-wing Deutsche Reichspartei mustered only 1 per cent of the popular vote last September. Also the similarly nationalistic Refugee party failed to obtain any seats this time. Anti-Semitism, on which the Nazi propaganda had prospered, seems to be no big drawing card any more; infrequent examples of it should not be exaggerated.

On the other extreme, the Communists, now suppressed, had only 2.2 per cent of the vote in 1953, whereas they had won 16 per cent in the elections of November 1932. The people of the Bonn Republic know only too well how their East German brethren suffer under Walter Ulbricht's yoke, and thus are immune to communism.

Last but not least, the armed forces have ceased to enjoy an independent existence which ambitious politicians in uniform might abuse. . . . The present Bonn Defense Minister, Franz Joseph Strauss, has made it crystal clear to his generals that he is their boss and that he will not tolerate disobedience.

Former Ambassador James B. Conant may be a bit too sanguine when proclaiming . . . that "we in the United States have in our new ally a powerful and reliable partner for the trying days that lie ahead." But I dare to hope that, unless an unforeseeable emergency arises, the German youth of today will be spared a repetition of that tragedy which befell its elders in 1933.

II. WEST GERMANY—ECONOMIC AND POLITICAL RECOVERY

EDITOR'S INTRODUCTION

Of all the problems West Germany has faced, the one it has mastered most successfully has been that of economic recovery. The West German economic comeback after the devastation of war has been the wonder of Europe. This development is dealt with in several articles at the outset of this section after a statement from the Chancellor of the Federal Republic, Konrad Adenauer, who comments on his country's economic recovery and more generally on his government's policies both domestic and foreign.

Most of these articles are factual reports about how and what has been accomplished in reviving Germany's economy. "Fruits of Economic Recovery" expresses the opinion held quite generally that the Adenauer government owes its continuance in power to the remarkable economic upturn. Next, *Business Week* credits Germany's central bank with a key role in the economic revival. A New York *Times* correspondent points to a problem that has often exercised Americans—that of cartelization or concentration in German industry which now appears to be under way again despite attempts by the victorious Allies after the war to break up the great German industrial combines which, it is generally conceded, backed Hitler's rise to power. Next, the same reporter notes Germany's growing ability to provide economic aid to underdeveloped countries outside Europe.

One problem which still remains, and is even increasing in seriousness, is the never ending flow of refugees from Communist-controlled East Germany. In 1958, for the fifth year, more than 200,000 East Germans sought refuge west of the Iron Curtain. The facts about this migration are set forth briefly in "Refugees from the East." (Further information on this problem is given in Section III, as the facts about the refugees tell much of the story of East Germany.) One way in which Germany's Nazi past is being dealt with is briefly noted in a dispatch from another New York *Times* correspondent. This is followed by an account of West Germany's emerging army and some of the problems posed by the remilitarization of Germany.

The section closes with four articles on the political party scene in the Federal Republic. Two major parties have dominated the political life of the West Germans since the November 1957 elections. This is in contrast to earlier years when many parties contested for votes, and to the interwar period when a multiparty system also held sway in the Weimar Republic. Most students believe this change heralds a fruitful trend for democracy in Germany. The November 1957 elections were also important for other reasons, as Louise M. Holborn notes in "Victory for Adenauer."

Following the elections the two major parties have, of course, continued political debate. Both seek a reunified Germany, though they propose somewhat different routes to this end. Post-election statements of both parties are given next. The last article discusses an election in northwest Germany which took place in mid-1958. There the issue of foreign policy was fought out more squarely than was the case, most observers feel, in the fall elections of the previous year, and again Adenauer supporters were returned. But the article also deals with a significant subject of debate in Germany, namely, whether the nation should become involved in atomic rearmament. This, of course, relates directly to West Germany's foreign policies—a question which is also important to Europe and East-West relations in general and which is dealt with in the last section of this book.

GERMANY TODAY AND TOMORROW [1]

Twelve years after the most complete collapse in their history the Germans—those who are living in freedom—have laid the

[1] By Konrad Adenauer, Chancellor of the Federal Republic of Germany. Translated by Rudolf Ernst. Published in a supplement, "Perspective of Germany," in the *Atlantic Monthly*. 200:110-13. March 1957. Reprinted by permission of Intercultural Publications, Inc.

foundations of their material existence anew. At the same time they have completed the restoration of a democratic state based upon law—a state which is aware of its obligations to its citizens and to other states.

Twice within three decades Germany has experienced the catastrophe of military defeat. For twelve years her people lived in totalitarian bondage. They have felt the consequences of this bondage in all their gravity and have learned from bitter experience to appreciate the value of freedom, justice, and peace as the highest good. But 17 million Germans in the Soviet-occupied zone of our nation still lack the blessings of personal freedom and a state based upon civil liberty.

These few recollections of the recent German past make it clear why there exists no extremism whatsoever in the Federal Republic of Germany, be it from the right or from the left. German labor has shown an extraordinary maturity even in days of distress—and we really knew distress in the first postwar years. Then, as today, labor clearly and decisively rejected all enticements of bolshevism. Radicalism from the right as well, as it is embodied in an exaggerated nationalism, is dead in the Federal Republic. This has been demonstrated by all our elections since the war.

Fragmentation of political parties—one of the reasons for the demise of the Weimar Republic—presents no actual danger in the Federal Republic. This state of affairs, largely attributable to the structure of our constitution, has resulted in a stability which has characterized our political activity to the present day. It is my contention that we have known how to exploit this stability. A consolidated domestic policy gave us an opportunity to integrate the Federal Republic into the community of free nations systematically and in line with the existing possibilities. Today the Federal Republic is a partner with equal rights in this community. The road we have had to take was long and often beset with difficulties. However, we have succeeded in reaching important goals.

When, on September 15, 1949, I was first elected Federal Chancellor by the Parliament, I stated, "Franco-German relations are the pivotal point of any European unification. I supported this view as early as twenty-five years ago." With the coming into force of the Paris Treaties, with the admission of the Federal Republic into the Western European Union and into NATO, we have become allies of France. This demonstrates how much Franco-German relations have changed since the founding of the Federal Republic. With the signing of the Saar Treaty, the last existing controversial issue between France and Germany has been eliminated. Thus, what I had hoped for seven years ago in our own self-interest and in the interest of Europe and of the whole free world, and what I have tried to achieve since, has become a reality.

As a member of NATO the Federal Republic has assumed the obligation to share in the defense of the free world. We stand by our word. We were faced with the task of setting up in a relatively short time a modern and efficient army after eleven years of being completely unarmed. Therefore we had to start from scratch. Furthermore, the armament policy of all nations is undergoing a process of revolutionary change owing to the breathtaking speed of the development of nuclear weapons and the continuous perfecting of conventional arms. These two factors could not fail to have a certain influence on the planning of the federal government. As was to be expected, we had to face purely technical as well as psychological difficulties. The build-up of armed forces could not reach, in all phases, the originally planned goals. But the meaning of such delays must be properly evaluated. The Federal Republic does not by any means intend to evade those obligations it assumed upon entering NATO. In arriving at pertinent decisions we are fully aware that the setting up of a combat-ready, efficient armed force as early as possible increases, above all, our own security. Only through complete solidarity with the other members of NATO can we effectively protect the freedom without which life would be intolerable.

Economic Recovery

Our contribution to the defense of the free world would rest upon weak foundations, however, had it not been possible to consolidate the economic and social structure of the Federal Republic as well. The achievement in these fields can be properly evaluated only if one recalls the conditions under which we had to reconstruct our economy after the war. We were compelled to start reconstruction in a state of complete devastation and with a productive capacity largely destroyed through the effects of war. We found ourselves isolated from the world economy and had a largely useless currency. Gratefully we remember the aid we received in those difficult times from those countries which only shortly before had been our enemies. Among them the United States took a leading position. Without this help it is very likely that we would not have been able to prevent total chaos. Then came the Marshall Plan. It gave us the chance to close many gaps which the war had left in our productive plant and to get the productive process under way again. But primary credit must be given to the initiative of German management and the unflagging assiduity of German labor; it was because of their efforts that the stimuli given by Marshall aid could be fully utilized.

Another important factor in our economic recovery was the currency reform of 1948. And the "social market economy"— the policy which has determined economic decisions of the federal government since its founding in 1949—played a major part in our rapid recovery, in that it opened the way for free enterprise. It proved possible to normalize the labor situation in a relatively short time, even though millions of people expelled from German territories behind the Oder-Neisse Line and from eastern and southeastern Europe poured into the Federal Republic. At present there is full employment in West Germany.

This far-reaching economic and financial recovery made it possible for us to tackle urgent social problems resulting from the war and to proceed with their solution. It was necessary— to mention only the most important problems—to provide relief for the disabled, the widows, and the orphans. Many millions of dwellings had been either destroyed or heavily damaged. To mitigate the pressing housing shortage, especially in the cities, the fields of rubble had to be cleared as quickly as possible to make way for new construction. This would not have been feasible without extensive public assistance. It was also imperative to create a new existence for the 10 million expellees and refugees from the East. These unfortunate people had for the most part lost everything but their lives. Through the programs of "Immediate Aid" and "Equalization of Burdens," we tried to compensate for at least a part of the property losses they had suffered. Priority aid was given to the most needy. Finally, West Berlin—separated from its natural hinterland and from its major marketing areas because of its isolated position within the Soviet-occupied zone—had to be granted assistance in order to enable the courageous population of this island surrounded by Communist totalitarianism to fight for the preservation of its freedom.

The Federal Republic fulfilled these tasks to the full extent of its means. It is true that we have not yet been able to remove the last vestiges of destruction wrought by the war—this would have exceeded our capabilities—but our policies have succeeded in removing the social and political tensions, the misery and want, which were bound to result from war, to such a degree that the fabric of society and the structure of the state have remained essentially intact. Today the federal government is continuing to realize its social program, which aims at relieving all insecurity arising from old age, sickness, and disablement. Major parts of this program have already been approved by Parliament.

Only a few years ago there were widespread fears that the Federal Republic might be an element of unrest and a source of permanent concern within the free world, in that the forces of domestic stability might be found inadequate. Today it is clear that these fears were unfounded. The Federal Republic now holds a position in Europe and in the free world which enables it itself to be a factor of stability within this community.

Unity of Germany and Europe

We still face a number of unsolved problems of momentous import. Whether and how it will be possible to settle them will determine the position of the Federal Republic in Europe and in the free world in the near future.

First of all, from the time of its establishment in 1949 we have always been aware, and we will continue to face the fact, that our state is only provisional. The Federal Republic is that part of Germany in which the people, with a guarantee of civil liberties, are in a position to express their political will through free elections. Therefore, the Federal Republic claims the right to represent politically the whole German people. The free world has acknowledged this right. However, we cannot forget that in the Soviet-occupied zone of Germany 17 million Germans have been denied all freedom. The preservation of our freedom and the reestablishment of German unity in peace and liberty is the supreme goal of our policy. Only reunification will secure stability for all Europe. We are striving for reunification in freedom. This implies that free elections in the whole of Germany are the first step in the process of reunification and that the all-German Parliament chosen by these elections can then freely decide the future constitutional and international status of our country. On these points we cannot make concessions; to do so would be to give up the principle of reunification in freedom.

In the first half of the twentieth century the German people twice experienced the horrors of war. We know that a third World War would jeopardize the survival of Germany and of Europe as well. This knowledge makes us realize the necessity of contributing in every possible way to the maintenance of peace. Therefore, a reunified Germany will not become a threat to anyone, for it will respect the security needs of all its neighbors, including those of the East European nations.

While in Moscow in September 1955, I declared, "Peace, whose preservation is the concern of all Germans, is the highest good. Therefore, you will find no one in Germany, neither among responsible politicians nor throughout the entire community, who even trifles with the idea that any of the great political problems awaiting solution can be solved by war." My view of that time continues to be the guiding principle of our foreign policy.

Besides the reunification of Germany we consider the unity of Europe one of the basic principles of our policy. The rise of the nation-state was one of the main causes for the fragmentation which has characterized the development of the European political structure during the past hundred years. We must supersede the concept of the nation-state if Europe is to become again an organic whole and to exert the political influence it deserves in the light of its history, traditions, and achievements. For that reason we have gladly accepted the proposals made by other countries for the integration of Europe and have done whatever we could toward their realization. This is especially true for the Coal and Steel Community and for the European Defense Community. In both cases the intention was to take the first steps toward broader European cooperation. EDC was to be developed into a European political community, the Coal and Steel Community into an over-all economic union. In both cases we were convinced that the number of participating countries would have to be increased. Then the European Defense Community was replaced by the Western European Union (WEU)—an expansion of the international organization set up under the Brussels Treaty of 1948—and by the direct incorporation of the Federal Republic into NATO. Only recently we have been making special efforts to extend the activities of the Coal and Steel Community through proposals to include more types of goods in the common market among the signatory states. . . .

Postwar developments and political changes compel us to regard the integration of Europe not only in its intra-European but also in its world-wide political and economic ramifications. The political and economic hegemony of Europe is a thing of the past. European civilization will maintain its position only if we activate it so as to meet prevailing conditions and if we are ready to defend it. . . .

I am convinced that our goals are essentially identical with those of the United States. John Foster Dulles as early as 1948 declared it necessary that Europe unite and develop a strength of its own. That is also our goal. I hope from the bottom of my heart that the Germany of tomorrow will be a unified and free

Germany, able to perform important functions within the European union and making its full contribution to the peace and welfare of the whole world.

ECONOMIC RESURGENCE [2]

It was only twelve years ago that West Germany was prostrate. All larger cities lay in ruins. Destroyed bridges blocked river transport. Railroads were knocked out. Mail service had stopped. Millions of Germans and people displaced from other countries wandered through the wreckage in search of family members, shelter and food. The daily diet in the first winter after surrender was down to less than half the normal intake. Fuel was lacking. Money had become almost worthless.

When the war ended in 1945, nobody would have predicted that West Germany twelve years later would be the leading industrial nation of Europe, its finances so sound that it would help to serve as a banker for the victors—Great Britain and France.

Today West Germany ranks first in the world as an exporter of automobiles, second only to the United States as an exporter of machinery, and behind only the United States and Britain as an exporter of electrical materials and chemicals.

Almost all evidence of war destruction is gone in the West Germany that came under control of the Western Allies. In the East, under Soviet control, all remains a shambles. Eastern Germany still is a place of rubble, ruins and poverty.

How Was It Done?

What lies back of the miracle of reconstruction in West Germany? How has a nation that still lay in ruins only eight years ago fully recovered and gone on to achievements greater than any in the past?

[2] From "Germany: From Rubble to Riches in 12 Years." *U.S. News & World Report.* p48+. September 20, 1957. Reprinted from *U.S. News & World Report,* an independent weekly news magazine published at Washington. Copyright 1957 United States News Publishing Corporation.

Then, too, how were 5.5 million new jobs created, and 11.8 million refugees from the East absorbed by the expanding German economy? It's as though the Eastern part of the United States, with its 80 million inhabitants, had absorbed 24 million people from the South and West after a national disaster.

Answers to questions about Germany's sensational recovery are varied and complicated.

The West Germany of today is made up of only 52 per cent of the area and 57 per cent of the population of the prewar nation. When this nation was split down the middle, its prewar economy torn completely apart, there was the problem of replacing lost production links and sources of materials.

Moreover, during the first three years after the war, the policy of Western powers was to hold down production and initiative to prevent any rebuilding of Germany's industrial potential. Western occupation forces were not supposed to do anything more than keep order and oversee distribution of relief aid to keep people alive.

It was only after the West realized, starting in 1948, that the Russians were draining all they could out of their part of Germany that the West Germans were permitted to start rebuilding. Without this go-ahead, the United States would have had to foot the bill for reparations owed by Germany to the Soviet Union to keep the Germans from being starved out—and probably falling prey to Communist infiltration.

American aid, raised to substantial amounts under the Marshall Plan in 1948, laid the foundation for recovery. Food and raw materials shipped in by the United States provided just what the Germans needed to launch a comeback. Brains and effort on the part of the Germans then got to work. The $3.6 billion of United States aid provided to West Germany under various programs is generally regarded as the most successful investment made anywhere in postwar reconstruction.

Unshackling of Economy

A policy of free enterprise unleashed the constructive forces of private initiative and self-interest in the smashed country.

Until mid-1948, the West German economy had been shackled by rationing and a maze of government controls. Suddenly, the great bulk of these was lifted at one stroke.

Credit for that daring move, made over opposition of some occupation officials and many Germans, goes to Dr. Ludwig Erhard, the Minister of Economics. He acted on free-enterprise ideas that a group of German economists had reworked during twelve years of controls under Hitler.

Dr. Erhard timed decontrol to come as closely as possible to a drastic currency reform in 1948. The combination worked wonders from the start. There was an immediate surge of business activity. Overnight, empty shops were filled with commodities that before had been hoarded or hidden for barter deals. Money once again had meaning. A free market guided prices to more realistic levels. Debts had been reduced by 90 per cent. A policy of sound money received priority.

Germans, who had suffered two disastrous price inflations in a lifetime, since 1948 have placed all of their effort back of defense of the new currency. Exports came to be considered a national duty, since only by exports could the value of the mark be maintained.

Sound money and a free market that determined prices were basic to the whole story of West German recovery.

Pro-business policies under the chancellorship of Konrad Adenauer proved helpful, as well. Although income taxes were kept high, corporations were allowed rapid amortization of costs of new equipment. Exports received tax favors and credit guarantees by the government. A liberalized trade policy opened up foreign markets and made it easier to buy raw materials abroad. Budget surpluses were built up.

Even more important to the success story of West Germany was the determined drive and hard work of the German people. Overtime became the rule, not the exception. After regular work hours, many a German filled a second job or pitched in on clearing and rebuilding cities and factories. Managers worked straight through week ends. Old men stayed on far beyond retirement age. Millions of women took full-time jobs.

As for the 11.8 million refugees from the East who crowded West German cities, they were a burden on the country at first, but in the long run they have turned out to be a distinct asset. Swelling the nation's population by a fourth, the refugees soon helped to boost production, too. In fact, the steep and prolonged rise in German output would have been impossible without the skill and effort of these transplanted Poles, Czechs, Hungarians, Yugoslavs and East Germans.

Labor-Industry Cooperation

One of the big changes that took place in postwar Germany, under the impetus of the drive for recovery, occurred in the trade unions. The unions, from the start, restrained their demands for wage increases and showed a willingness to await better times. Partly this was due to the over-supply of labor provided by the refugees. More important, there was a realization on the part of union leaders and workers alike that it was to the benefit of all to plow back as much of the early profits as possible into building up equipment and working capital.

As a result, little time has been lost on strikes in the last eight years. Now, with business flourishing, the years of restraint in the common cause are paying off. Wages and fringe benefits are increasing along with profits. Today, the German worker's family is better off than ever before.

Workers now own refrigerators, washing machines, television sets, motorcycles—even secondhand cars in a car market that is still short for export reasons. The big gap that once existed between the working class and the middle class is narrowing.

Throughout the story of Germany's comeback, the process of recovery has been speeded by an ability of the nation to turn problems into assets.

For example, consider what happened when the West Germans lost the high-cost but plentiful food surplus that used to come from East Germany. That loss, at least in the early postwar years, was viewed as a catastrophe. But very soon after things began to hum again, the Germans found that they could buy even cheaper food abroad in exchange for their manufactured goods.

Even bomb destruction and extensive dismantling of industry for reparations have worked out in Germany's favor. For one thing, these losses cleared the country of a lot of outmoded equipment. In place of the old machinery, plant after plant now operates more efficiently than ever before with the most modern equipment in Europe. Costs have been cut and productivity boosted.

What's more, the great demand for this new equipment helped Germany in other ways. It enabled capital-goods industries to grow faster than most other industries in the country. Thus, when the Korean War boom set in, German producers of equipment and machinery were ready to take on export orders at short delivery dates. That paved the way for an easy reentry to world markets, and German industrialists made the most of it.

A big advantage in the export drive was the fact that Germany had to bear no such burden of defense costs as the United States, Britain and France. Instead of making arms, German industrialists concentrated on peacetime machinery.

Today, as the world passes through its biggest investment boom—with old industrial nations modernizing their plants and agricultural nations pushing industrialization—the Germans are cashing in with a huge volume of orders. They find they can trade on particularly favorable terms—because the prices of raw materials and foodstuffs have declined since the Korean War, while prices of capital goods have stayed relatively high.

Only twelve years after a war that left the nation in ruins and bankrupt, West Germany is so rich that it is in the position of giving financial help to other countries—including two victors of World War II, Britain and France. It has extended $893 million in public credits to other European nations through the European Payments Union. In addition, Germany has made a $100 million credit to the World Bank, pledged the largest contribution to a proposed European development fund and aided victims of the Dutch flood and the Hungarian revolution.

The Deutsche Mark ranks as one of the world's hardest currencies. . . .

As foreign economists see it, West Germany is in for a gradual tapering off of the boom, now that the economy has grown so far so fast. But the West German economy is considered solid enough to weather any storm now in sight.

And yet, right next door to that thriving country, in East Germany, other Germans with the same skill and ability to work hard are still living among ruins. Enduring poverty and want, they have little chance of even beginning the kind of comeback the Western half of their onetime nation has made. Under communism they are deprived of the free market and the sound money that were so basic to the ruin-to-riches story of West Germany.

THE FRUITS OF ECONOMIC RECOVERY [3]

A ten-minute television film, shown during the [1957] campaign, brings alive the main reasons for the result of the September 15 general election in West Germany. It explains why a majority of the voters gave eighty-two-year-old Konrad Adenauer a longer term as chancellor than anyone else in German history except Bismarck.

The picture begins with a showing of the rubble to which Germany had been reduced at the war's end. It ends with shots of Germans, well nourished and neatly dressed, smugly driving their Volkswagens. By contrast, the camera is flashed on a French filling station where an attendant is politely telling a motorist, "Sorry, sir, no gas." As in the film, so at the polls; Herr Adenauer became Mr. Prosperity, and the voters approved his slogan of "No experiments."

The same electioneering picture goes on to show Chancellor Adenauer in the company of President Eisenhower, Secretary Dulles, and leaders of other Allied nations. It thus personifies the idea that, from their position as outcasts, the West Germans have been elevated and readmitted to the civilized community. The viewer was left in no doubt that it is to Chancellor Adenauer that he owes his regained respectability. The combination of well-being and membership in the best club impelled the electorate to give Adenauer an absolute majority of 43 seats in the 497-member parliament.

[3] From "Atlantic Report on the World Today—Germany." *Atlantic Monthly.* 200:12+. December 1957. Reprinted by permission.

There are a couple of other reasons for the spectacular success of Adenauer's Christian Democratic Party at the polls. The Socialists failed to offer a dynamic program and mustered as their leader only an amiable mediocrity named Erich Ollenhauer. They renounced socialism. They spoke fuzzily of some state control over basic industry. They abandoned the demand for nationalization of coal and steel. They embraced private enterprise. They proclaimed their attachment to NATO and to the West.

Finally, the Chancellor must credit the Russians with a share in his electoral success. Stumping the country, Adenauer kept telling the people he was crusading for Christianity against communism. At the same time Nikita Khrushchev was touring East Germany under the auspices of the Red government there and shouting that Adenauer was a warmonger and an American stooge. Many Germans saw in Khrushchev's behavior a confirmation of Adenauer's claim that he was defending the faith against the infidels.

How Much Recovery?

The economic comeback in West Germany is genuine. The construction of 4.2 million dwelling units in the past eight years is phenomenal. About 16 million West Germans, or one of every three inhabitants, have moved into new homes. It is a monument to hard work and capable organization. Together with the abundance of consumer goods, it makes West Germany a capitalist window exhibit, contrasting with the ramshackle conditions in Communist East Germany.

Statistics describing advances in the German Republic are impressive but on close scrutiny perhaps misleading. As an illustration, take wages. From 1950 to 1956 the pay in the West German worker's envelope grew 57 per cent in cash or, after discounting the rise in prices, 35 per cent in purchasing power. This headway, while noteworthy, falls into truer perspective when one realizes that German wages are below those in Britain and in some continental European countries. Excepting rent—which is important—the cost of living in West Germany is not far below that in the United States. Yet in German industry the average pay is the equivalent of less than $25 per week.

This, in turn, is a factor in the low production costs which enabled the German Republic to push its exports this year to some $9 billion. West Germany has more than doubled its share of world trade in the past seven years. Unemployment has shrunk from 10 per cent of the labor force in 1949 to 2.1 per cent today. The pendulum is even swinging toward a serious shortage of workers. Another plus in the German economy—though it also has disadvantages—is the hoard of $6 billion in foreign currency and gold.

Consumption has risen sharply. West Germans are eating and drinking twice as much beef, milk, beer, and wine as they were eight years ago; thrice the fats, fourfold the pork, eggs, coffee, and tea. They are smoking twice as many cigarettes.

All these and many other figures appear in a different light when one recalls the dismally low level from which the ascent started. If the number of American women wearing stockings were to increase twenty times in seven years, it would be something of an economic miracle because so large a proportion of ladies in the United States already wear them. The actual twenty-fold rise of feminine consumption of stockings in West Germany since 1949 means very much less, indeed, because hardly any German women could afford them a few years ago.

The same applies to the increase by two and a half times of West German industrial production in the corresponding period. Stories in the American press have been indicating that the German Republic is already the foremost economic power across the Atlantic. It is being suggested that the West German economy has been showing its heels to Britain. In fact the Germans have passed the British in steel, of which they are manufacturing almost 25 million tons a year, compared to Britain's 20.6 million. In most other essentials, however, the British are still ahead. With roughly the same-sized populations, Britain's gross national product is about $54 billion a year, West Germany's $46 billion.

Tight Money

There are defects in the economy which may retard growth. The principal weakness is shortage of liquid capital. German industry has been plowing back into plant expansion and modernization about 44 per cent of its profits. Moreover, stiff corporate and individual taxes have enriched the state but limited the capital at the disposal of firms and persons. Finally, people have been putting extra money into savings deposits which the banks are willing to transform into loans only at prohibitive interest rates.

As a result, many German companies have such scant liquid reserves of capital that they could not stand a few months of slack business. Even concerns free of debts can slither to the brink of insolvency, as happened this fall to the big Henschel locomotive and truck firm. It desperately appealed to the banks for help when it had to meet the payroll for its 10,000 employees while $2.5 million worth of trucks remained unsold in its warehouses.

West Germany's tight money market has so far restricted the export of capital. Considering its high degree of industrialization, this nation is playing a trivial part in the undeveloped countries of Asia, Africa, and the Middle East. Yet that will probably change. Part of the West German Central Bank's vast foreign exchange hoard may be released for the purpose.

This reserve is a form of insurance, since it could pay for German imports over an eight-month period. But it is not an unmixed blessing. More than half of the recent flow of sterling, dollars, Swiss francs, and other currencies has lately been entering Germany as a gamble on an upward revaluation of the Deutsche Mark. Foreigners could withdraw their funds as suddenly as they poured them in. Many recollect that withdrawal of alien capital was a major factor in the dreadful business crash in Germany in 1931. . . .

Another flaw in the economy is West Germany's lag in developing the atom, radar, aircraft, automation, and standardization. The Germans have lost their lead in scientific education. Professor Leo Brandt, deputy chief of the German Atomic Committee, discusses these deficiencies in his book, *The Second Industrial Revolution.*

He contrasts the small number of atomic physicists being trained in the German Republic with the 2000 a year being graduated in Russia, and he compares the handful of mechanical engineers being educated in Germany with the 200,000 to be turned out annually at Soviet universities from 1960 on. The German professor remarks that 14 per cent of German students are receiving tuition-free scholarships, compared with 70 per cent in Britain.

ROLE OF THE CENTRAL BANK [4]

Germany's recovery from the ruins of World War II to its present position as the most prosperous country in Europe has been the subject of a great deal of study and discussion. One expert on the question, Professor Henry C. Wallich of Yale University, made a new contribution with a study that credits the Bank Deutscher Laender, Germany's central bank, with a crucial role in the revival of the German economy.

In coming to this conclusion, Wallich implies that Germany's orthodox monetary policy, carried out by a central bank independent of the government, should serve as an example to other nations. In saying this, he is bolstering the position of the United States Federal Reserve, which has also favored independence and orthodoxy.

Last summer, the Bank Deutscher Laender became the Deutsche Bundesbank under a new law that was aimed at clarifying the relationship between the government and the bank. Under the law, the bank remains independent in carrying out its functions, but the government cannot take part in discussions of the bank's policies. The bank is supposed to "support the general economic policy" of the government as long as it is compatible with its own policy. Just what happens if there is a conflict is not spelled out.

As long as the present government is in power, no real conflicts are likely. For both the bank and the government have pursued the same policies in bringing about recovery.

Wallich makes clear that Germany possessed a number of other advantages that aided recovery—the influx of cheap refugee

[4] From "Bank Gets Credit for German Revival." *Business Week.* p65. March 29, 1958. Reprinted from the March 29, 1958 issue of *Business Week* by special permission. Copyrighted © 1958 by the McGraw-Hill Publishing Company, Inc.

labor from East Germany, the lack of a heavy rearmament burden, the cooperative attitude of labor. In addition, Germany received big doses of foreign aid, and her people showed a "willingness" to "work hard in order to make good war losses."

Wallich states that these advantages would have been dissipated if the government and the central bank had not followed "deliberate policies" aimed at assuring both recovery and monetary stability. The government managed to achieve budgetary surpluses that helped to spur investment. Wallich reports that 42.2 per cent of total investment came from business itself, 21.8 per cent from consumer savings, and 35.9 per cent from the government. Only 29.2 per cent of surplus government funds went into government investment; the remaining 70.8 per cent was diverted into business investment and housing.

But it was the central bank's policies that created the environment for expansion, says Wallich. Although it was independent of the government, it shared the same aims: to raise output of the domestic economy and to stimulate international trade.

From the beginning, the bank took an orthodox view. It did not follow the easy money policies of other European countries, which pumped credit into the economy to spur investment and production, and used import controls and export subsidies to keep international payments in balance. Instead, the German bank deliberately aimed at maintaining a stable currency and freeing trade from controls.

The bank's decision was motivated, in part, by Germany's earlier ruinous inflations. It felt that a stable currency would be the key to reviving exports.

PROBLEM OF INDUSTRIAL COMBINES [5]

The West German government . . . [has] urged that it be freed of its obligation to break up mammoth industrial combinations.

The United States, British and French Governments, which formerly occupied West Germany, promulgated these laws on the

[5] From "Bonn Would Drop Anti-Cartel Law," by M. S. Handler, correspondent. New York *Times*. p4. May 3, 1958. Reprinted by permission.

assumption that big industrial combinations were incompatible with a peaceful Germany. The West German government committed itself to take over enforcement of the deconcentration laws when it acquired sovereignty May 5, 1955.

Under these laws such giant concerns as the Krupp Works, I. G. Farben Industrie, and the United Steel Works were broken up or were obliged, as in the case of the Krupp concern, to agree to sell their iron, steel and mining properties.

The Krupp concern, for example, was told to sell the great Rheinhausen Steel Works by 1959 but there does not appear to be any likelihood that this will be done. The Krupp concern has been conducting a campaign for permission to reintegrate the Rheinhausen Steel Works as a directly controlled operational unit.

Last year [1957] Chancellor Konrad Adenauer asked the former occupation powers to be excused from carrying out the deconcentration laws.

The Western Allies replied with a request for a progress report on what the West German government had done in carrying out its commitment. . . .

The trend toward a reconcentration of heavy industry and banking has become so pronounced in recent years that the West German government feels the law no longer can be enforced without trying to turn back the clock.

The reconcentration into big industrial combinations has been particularly noticeable in steel and banking. In the latter field three great commercial banks now hold the lead in West Germany. This regrouping was finally achieved through phased mergers of the smaller institutions into which the big pre-war banks had been broken up.

Western Allied officials in West Germany are inclined to share the view that the time is gone when a reconcentration of heavy industry can or should be prevented. Economic trends in the Western world indicate that this is an era of big industrial combinations, they say.

The Western Allies' officials also say privately that the deconcentration laws were promulgated when Germany was an occupied enemy state. West Germany is now an ally and a member of the Western camp and cannot be subjected to special economic restrictions that might have served a useful purpose immediately after the end of World War II, these officials contend.

The private view is that the deconcentration laws are dead since they are not enforceable under present conditions.

[At the end of January 1959, the Krupp combine made known its intention of regrouping certain of its coal and steel properties, having been unable to sell them, it claimed. No immediate objections were heard from Western governments which earlier had insisted on decartelization of the industrial combines in Western Germany.—Ed.]

GERMANY AND THE WORLD ECONOMY [6]

West German industrial power consolidated its position in 1957 as the backbone of the West European economic structure.

In terms of production, trade and future capabilities, it exercised an increasing force of attraction upon its continental neighbors, both West and East, and was wooed with remarkable persistence by the underdeveloped countries of the Middle East, South and Southeast Asia.

In other words, West Germany has duplicated the feat of United States industry in relation to the economy of the rest of the world and has become the second pole of attraction for countries needing industrial development equipment.

The Ruhr has become a magnet for trade missions from many parts of the world, as West Germany is more actively represented in overseas development programs than any other country except America.

German engineering projects—harbor development, railroads, hydroelectric plants, steel and cement mills and many others—are being built in the underdeveloped areas.

This special position was not won without financial risk, since many of the projects involve credits to countries suffering from chronic trade deficits from investments exceeding their normal capacity to pay. India, Turkey are cases in point.

[6] From "Bonn's Strength Spreads in World," by M. S. Handler, correspondent. New York *Times*. p49. January 7, 1958. Reprinted by permission.

The financial risks have been shared out in the industrial-banking consortiums concerned in these projects. It is a rare West German concern that is prepared to assume the full responsibility for financing an overseas project.

The position of German industry in Europe developed several interesting characteristics. The huge surpluses with the European Payments Union, while gratifying to the pride of the Germans, also filled them with a certain amount of concern. The growing indebtedness of France and Britain, for example, tended to create an unhealthy trading position in which the inevitable threats of protectionism were uttered by the debtor countries.

A normal way of reducing surpluses would be to increase imports and the export of capital. The government did in effect increase imports somewhat but with little effect on the surplus balance. The export of capital was quite unimportant in 1957. Small investments were made overseas, 200 million florins' worth of Dutch Treasury bills were purchased in November. Anticipated repayments on the London debt agreement were made. The total effect was almost nil.

As exporters of high-priced industrial equipment the West Germans are still enjoying a temporary advantage in importing raw materials, the prices of which have been falling. Declining freight rates also have been advantageous. As long as the imbalance between industrial and raw material prices continues without a breakdown in the world markets, it is thought unlikely the West Germans will be able to deal effectively with their surplus position in the European Payments Union.

Armament orders placed in Britain, France and Italy were of insufficient volume to reduce the position, although the West German government has been holding out this hope to the debtor countries.

Caught in this difficult situation, major corporations in France, Belgium and Italy began to court German concerns with offers of cooperation. Leading West German concerns and banks received flattering invitations to send study missions, cost free, to visit plants in the three countries.

The Eastern European countries, the Soviet Union and Poland in particular, have been pressing to get into the German market in a big way. . . .

The Bonn government and semi-official trade organizations still say there is no pressing need for an important penetration into the Eastern markets. Their contention is that the pattern of West German trade precludes resumption of Eastern trade relations on the scale of the early 1930's.

Despite these public assertions, there does seem to be a growing interest in the Soviet-controlled markets. Individual traders have increased their volume in these markets. [West Germany in April 1958 concluded a trade agreement with the Soviet Union for a two-way exchange of goods valued at $7.5 million to take place before the end of 1960.—Ed.]

THE REFUGEE PROBLEM [7]

Each day, on an average, seven hundred persons [leave East Germany and flee to West Berlin and West Germany]. . . .

The saying among Germans is that these people from the East, fleeing from communism, are "voting with their feet."

Many of today's "voters" are school teachers, college professors, doctors. In some cases, whole classes of students with their teachers have crossed the line. Many of today's refugees are running from pressure exerted by Moscow's puppet regime to impose Communist doctrine in the field of education and the professions.

Over a nine-year period from September 1949, when regular statistics first were started on refugees, until August 1958, more than 2.1 million persons have fled from East Germany. Another million or so got out earlier, in the four years immediately following World War II. Far from tapering off in recent years, the number of persons involved in the flight from communism has been on the increase, as the Reds have made one move after another to tighten their grip on East Germany.

[7] From "12 Years Under Communism And Still They Flee." *U.S. News & World Report*. 45:85. September 26, 1958. Reprinted from *U.S. News & World Report*, an independent weekly news magazine published at Washington. Copyright 1958. United States News Publishing Corporation.

Today the main escape route is no longer the border area of West Germany but the dividing line between the east and west sectors of Greater Berlin. The Communists made the direct route of flight to West Germany tougher by tightening up on passports for people wishing to "visit relatives" or "do business." In addition, Red border guards have been reinforced in forests along the frontier. In Berlin, on the other hand, there's still free movement throughout the city.

East Germans wanting to flee with a minimum risk of detection go to West Berlin and there join the hundreds of thousands of people who cross the city every day to work, shop, take in the movies or go to the opera. . . .

Among those involved in this mass flight from communism are people of all ages and from every walk of life. Whole families leave their homes and communities to get out from under Red pressure. Recently, a prominent band leader and his musicians fled west because they clashed with Communist restrictions on jazz. The refugees include lawyers, acrobats, storekeepers, writers, policemen.

Industrial workers and craftsmen, a favored class in Communist countries, make up the largest single group of refugees. A total of 18,888 workers and artisans fled west in the first half of this year, following tens of thousands who left Red factories earlier.

Students are streaming out of East Germany by the thousands—most of them because they were frustrated by Communist restrictions on who can and who cannot receive higher education. Under the Reds, children of middle-class parents have little chance of being admitted to universities and higher technical schools. Priority is given to children of party officials, intellectuals and workers.

On top of this, Red authorities recently decreed that students, to qualify for higher schooling, must take an oath of nonbelief in any religious faith. This only served to step up the flight of students westward. In the last year, one fourth of all high-school seniors in East Germany have fled from the country.

The most striking thing about the present upswing in the number of refugees is that it includes large numbers of professional men and intellectuals—two groups that have long enjoyed high earnings and special treatment under the Communists. These are people who were favored by Red authorities because their skilled services were badly needed: doctors, professors, engineers, teachers, scientists. Recently, however, even they have come under heavy Communist pressure.

Doctors suddenly have been pressed to join collective farms as government employees. Physicians caring for industrial workers have found that sick leaves they grant are canceled by bureaucrats to cut absenteeism. Lawyers, after tangling with Red justice on behalf of private clients, are being asked to drop private practice entirely. Engineers find they must sign so-called peace resolutions, even spy on workers suspected of anti-Communist sympathies.

So far this year, 2,393 teachers and professors have sought asylum in West Germany. They found teaching more and more difficult under Communist pressures to curtail academic freedom and inject the Marxist-Leninist line into history, economics, philosophy, law and even the natural sciences.

All of this loss of skills and manpower is a source of growing worry to East German authorities. It worries Moscow, too, for the Russians count on industries in this satellite state to supply many finished products. In fact, East Germany is, next to Red China, Russia's largest trading partner.

Of the 3 million persons who have fled East Germany since World War II, almost three fourths have been of working age.

Red authorities—their industry already lagging because of labor shortages—are trying to stop the flight of precious manpower out of East Germany in all sorts of ways. Banks must report immediately large withdrawals from private accounts, as a possible tipoff to escape plans. Police and informers travel all trains between the Berlins. . . .

West Germany—fantastically busy and prosperous when compared with the East—has gained enormously from the steady stream of skilled and educated refugees. Indeed, officials in

Bonn say the country's recovery from war and the development of its industries over the last decade could not have been as great as it was without the flow of East Germans into the labor force.

Jobs are not as plentiful in the West now as they once were. Even so, engineers, technicians and skilled workers from the East are usually able to find work.

The Bonn government is working overtime to resettle all refugees. There are special-assistance programs. High school students, for example, get government aid so they can continue their studies. But not all the refugees are so fortunate. Older people, particularly if they have no relatives in West Germany, often have to spend weeks in refugee camps before they find new homes.

For East Germans, the flight to the West is a momentous decision. Running away means giving up their homes, all their possessions, often their friends and relatives, for the uncertain life in a refugee barracks. Nevertheless, they choose that to life under the Communists. The trek out began as soon as the Communists took over. It has never stopped. Right now it is on the rise—with as many as one thousand Germans a day turning their backs on the homes they have always known to start life anew in the freedom and opportunity of the West.

HANDLING THE NAZI PAST [8]

A history institute [in Munich] is waging war on a tendency of some Germans to smooth over the faults of the Third Reich and make a Napoleon out of Hitler.

The Munich Institute for Current History, which specializes in making known the facts about the Nazi period, is supported by the federal government and all the states of West Germany.

Dr. Helmut Krausnick, deputy director of the institute and editor of its quarterly publication, says he encounters from time to time Germans who excuse and exalt Hitler. "You mean

[8] From "Nazi Data Bared By Unit in Munich," by Harry Gilroy, correspondent. New York *Times*. p14. August 10, 1958. Reprinted by permission.

he was a great statesman although a gangster," the historian replies.

It is Dr. Krausnick's belief that the work of the institute is playing an important part in giving to both the older generation and the one now in school a true picture of the Hitler period. But he also feels that many teachers at present tread lightly on this subject.

"Teachers say there are no texts or documents available on which to base lessons on the subject, but this is not true," he said. He himself has put out a book on the Nazi period. The book was started by Professor Hermann Mau, first director of the institute, and completed by Dr. Krausnick.

Apart from that book, the institute has published ten volumes on aspects of the Third Reich and in its quarterly has reproduced many basic Nazi documents. Next month it will print the diary of the commandant of the infamous Auschwitz concentration camps.

The quarterly publication has two thousand subscribers, including public officials, editors, writers and scholars. The West German press and radio often quote from documents printed in it. Politicians have used the material to combat neo-Nazi groups.

Dr. Krausnick has appeared in court proceedings to give jurors background on such matters as the Nazi government policy on concentration camps.

"There are many people who pass over discreditable things they saw, and still cling to the belief that there must have been a sense of order at the top," he said. "We have been called to show that Hitler knew what was going on and wanted it that way."

The institute is frequently asked to supply lecturers for conferences of teachers and public forums. One request on Dr. Krausnick's desk today was from the commander of the German Army officers' school in Munich, asking that the young officers be given an unromanticized picture of the Third Reich.

There are eight scientific members of the institute and a varying number of collaborators. They work with forty thousand books covering the Hitler period, official government and party publications of the time, proceedings of the trials held after 1945 and fifteen hundred depositions made by Nazis on all levels.

THE NEW GERMAN ARMY [9]

If we are to treat Germany as an ally, she must be a full ally with rights as well as responsibilities. Strategical experts say there can be no Western defense without German participation. Therefore such participation must be made efficient. This is a calculated risk. But when one looks eastward at the Soviet Union and its satellite helots no alternative appears—until we can all agree on real disarmament.

Bonn's new army will be Western Europe's strongest, most modern and efficient. It will be equipped with missiles and nuclear weapons whose warheads, at least right now, remain under American control. Almost 60 per cent of its peacetime strength will be made up of professional soldiers.

The local armaments industry is recovering. The Germans are about to produce short-range guided missiles. Aircraft manufacturers are producing trainers and transports.

Bonn strives to emphasize a new philosophical role for its forces. They are controlled by civilians—the president, the chancellor and defense minister. A standing parliamentary committee so far supervises every move. It is contended these soldiers are "civilians," not "subjects," in uniform; that their function is not aggressive; that it is to protect Western freedom as well as the Fatherland.

Defense Minister Strauss claims: "If an East German rising occurs, I shall forbid any soldier in the Bundeswehr [the new army's name] to fire a single shot or assist the freedom fighters in any way." Could this really happen if a "Hungary" exploded in the Soviet zone?

There was much doubt here and abroad about the wisdom of giving atomic weapons to the Bundeswehr. Many Germans still fear this might make of their country a nuclear battlefield

[9] From "West Germany and Nuclear Arms," by C. L. Sulzberger, foreign affairs columnist. New York *Times*. p18. May 3, 1958. Reprinted by permission.

if ever there is a war. But as both this Government and NATO see it, facts cannot be escaped. Everybody hopes for controlled international disarmament. Until that happens, it is argued, all alliance forces must be equally equipped.

This is especially true now that other allies are reneging on commitments. The French have withdrawn to Algeria most of the troops supposed to be stationed here. The British have broken their promise to maintain four divisions. Even we are paring our garrison. Germany's function . . . is therefore automatically increased. . . .

Bonn's General Staff reckons accordingly. If the Bundeswehr had no such arms, the Russians (in a war) would probe the forces opposite them, find the weakness, then break through, splitting the entire Allied front. The only way to rectify this situation would be to employ strategic nuclear bombs. Germany would be destroyed.

This is tricky logic. But it is evident the Federal Republic cannot play the major part in continental defense if it is equipped only with outmoded weapons. Once it became necessary to rearm this country, it became just as necessary to make the most modern matériel available.

Eventually Germany will have a permanent core of twelve fast-moving atomic divisions—under NATO. But beside them will be a national "territorial" army of unfixed strength and not under NATO. What will be its ultimate role—for example in a Soviet zone "Hungary" ?

Relatively soon the Federal Republic will have the most efficient military establishment between the United States and Russia. Then will this chastened, industrious people, now so ably and moderately led, remain content merely to bolster a Western coalition? Or will they strike out on a strong and independent basis?

In the latter event, would they be satisfied to remain neutral, a kind of super Switzerland or Sweden? Or might they place their regained power upon the diplomatic bargaining counter in Moscow?

VICTORY FOR ADENAUER [10]

The Federal Republic of Germany occupies a strong position in Europe today, with the most stable currency outside the dollar area and a strategic importance based on its manpower, its economic potential and its geographical situation. This position gives particular significance to the results of the election for its Bundestag (lower house) on September 15, 1957, which brought an overwhelming victory for the federal chancellor, Dr. Konrad Adenauer, and his party, the Christian Democratic Union (CDU) with its Bavarian affiliate, the Christian Social Union (CSU). In a remarkably high poll in which 82.24 per cent of the eligible voters participated, the CDU/CSU gained just over half the votes, as compared to 45.2 per cent in 1953, and elected 270 out of the 497 deputies, in place of 244 in 1953.

As important as the fact that the CDU/CSU gained the majority of the seats in the Bundestag for the first time since the Federal Republic was founded in 1949 is the disappearance of splinter parties, formerly so common in Germany. Although 13 parties presented candidates in the election, only 4 are represented in the Bundestag: the CDU/CSU, which forms the government; the chief opposition, the Social Democratic party (SPD), which won 169 seats (compared to 151 in 1953) and increased its percentage of the poll from 28.8 in 1953 to 31.8; the Free Democratic party (FDP), which declined from 48 to 41 seats; and the German party (DP), which elected 17 representatives, as compared to 15 in 1953. Most striking of the changes is that the Refugee party, which had 27 deputies in the last Bundestag, has none in the present House. None of the smaller parties secured either 5 per cent of the total votes or the 3 seats by direct votes in local districts which would have provided representation in the Bundestag. Thus Nazis and Communists have also vanished as political forces.

That both the CDU/CSU and the SPD increased their share of the votes and seats brings Germany closer to the two-party system than it has been since 1945. Moreover, the DP placed

[10] From "Adenauer's Victory: An Advance for Democracy?" article by Louise W. Holborn, professor of government at Connecticut College. *Foreign Policy Bulletin.* 37:25-6. November 1, 1957. Reprinted by permission.

its representatives in the Bundestag only by winning six seats in local districts, which was a result of its strong support by the CDU. The CDU seems to have gained votes from the small parties and the new voters (35 million eligible voters in 1957 as compared to 33 million in 1953). By contrast, the SPD seems to have gained only a small percentage of the new young voters on the rolls and failed to broaden its electoral support among the Catholic workers despite the fact that it campaigned on a liberal rather than a socialist program. The SPD's increase of votes came mainly from the 300,000 who formerly supported Dr. Heinemann's neutralist party (GVP), which dissolved in June 1957 when its leader joined the SPD, and from the 600,000 Communist voters who were instructed by their leaders to vote for the SPD. In the Bundestag the SPD, for the first time, now holds one third of the seats, which means that it can block any legislation aimed at revision of the constitution and also that it can have the Bundestag convened at its own initiative.

Why Adenauer Won

What accounts for the decisive renewal of Dr. Adenauer's mandate for a third time despite the widespread and sometimes bitter criticism of the government in the weeks before the election? At that time one heard much about the Chancellor's advanced age, his authoritarian handling of his cabinet and party colleagues, his unwillingness to take the opposition into his confidence, fear of Church interference in politics, and hopes for a more constructive approach to the reunification of Germany. Yet in the end more decisive factors influenced the electors.

Foremost among them was the "economic miracle": virtual full employment, record exports nearly a third higher than in 1954, a more or less successful fight with inflation and a stable currency. Meanwhile the opposition, the SPD, had shelved its traditional demand for nationalization of heavy industry, dropped its social reform program and evolved nothing so attractive as the government's remarkable increase of old-age pensions and promise of tax reductions. Even the trade unions which were not affiliated with particular parties asked their members to vote for the party which had done most for trade union interests.

In foreign affairs the government stood on its record: the winning of independence and subsequently of membership in NATO and the Western European Union. Though Adenauer's policy of strength and alignment with the West has not secured reunification, the Berlin Declaration of July 29, 1957 signed by the United States, Britain, France and Germany, recognizes the right of the German people to reestablish their national unity. In comparison the SPD proposal to ban nuclear weapons in Germany through a provision of the federal constitution and to create a European security system—including a demilitarized reunited Germany, which would be guaranteed by both the United States and the Soviet Union—appeared too vague and unrealistic to the voters. Moreover, the Soviet Union itself aided Dr. Adenauer's cause through its intransigence over the repatriation of German prisoners, as well as Khrushchev's violent attack on the Chancellor during his visit to East Berlin and his renewed refusal to discuss concretely the problem of reunification.

In the three elections since 1949 the German people have more and more voted conservative, but in the sense of conserving their newly built economic system within the framework of the Western community. The time is now at hand to transform what is a well-functioning state apparatus into a working democratic parliamentary system. The operations of the last Bundestag showed an encouraging degree of give-and-take in the legislative process between the government and opposition. The election campaign was quiet and reasonable, with many indications that the electorate prefers to see political issues argued on a higher plane. Perhaps above all, the elimination of the splinter and extremist parties, which have been the bane of German political life in the past, shows a substantial degree of maturity and political judgment on the part of the electorate. If the CDU uses its electoral victory to develop truly national policies in which all parties can feel they have a share, the 1957 election may mark a decisive step toward a genuine German democratic nationhood.

GOVERNMENT PARTY POLICIES [11]

The Christian Democratic Union (CDU), which together with its Bavarian affiliate, the Christian Socialist Union (CSU), has 270 of the 497 members in the present Bundestag and which has been the leading government party since the Bundestag's inception in 1949, held its Eighth Party Convention from September 18 to 21 [1958] at Kiel.

The convention was highlighted by . . . the unanimous adoption of an agenda for the party and a document known as the "Kiel Manifesto," in which the party formulated its foreign policy principles. . . .

[Following] are excerpts from the "Kiel Manifesto" adopted at the CDU Convention:

The Federal Party Convention once again repeats most emphatically that our liberty, the spiritual and cultural values of our life, and the economic and social development of our country can only be assured by steady adherence to the successful foreign policy of the federal government.

The Federal Party Convention therefore expects the federal government to continue with its policy of alliance within the framework of the Atlantic community. It expects a determined continuation of our European policy. The unification of Europe is and will continue to be one of the greatest tasks of our times. The future of the entire German people—on both sides of the zonal border—and that of all the other European peoples depends on this.

The reunification of Germany in freedom remains the aim of all our endeavors. It is the national duty of all Germans to advance it. For as long as the global political position does not permit of reunification, we must devote all our strength to the preservation and strengthening of personal and spiritual ties with the Germans on the other side of the zonal border.

[11] From "The 1958 CDU Convention." *The Bulletin*, issued by the Press and Information Office of the German Federal Government. 6:5. September 23, 1958.

The CDU "Agenda"

The CDU Convention set up an "Agenda," which among other things includes the following points as the politico-economic and socio-political aims of the party:

Continuation of the social market economy with the aim of constantly increasing the over-all output of national economy. Safeguarding the purchasing power of the currency;

Further extension of the legal safeguards of competitive output;

Realization without delay of the European Economic Community; no self-sufficient isolation from other partners in trade, in particular the creation of a system of agreements, such as is aimed at in the Free Trade Area;

Strengthening of the middle classes;

Revision of laws at present in force, in order to prevent excessive economic concentration;

Increased support for the construction of homes for families, in particular for young or prolific families;

Promotion of saving in every form;

Accelerated transfer of suitable industrial enterprises from public into private possession, distribution of shares to be as wide as possible;

Reform of health insurance;

Reform of accident insurance;

Acceleration of turnover tax reform with the aims of bringing about equality in competition;

Intensified promotion of measures in support of agriculture;

Elimination of the critical conditions at present prevailing in road traffic;

Advancement of schools, of education and upbringing, science and research.

The following resolution was also adopted:

The Party Convention of the Christian Democratic Union of Germany is shocked by the intolerable exacerbation of conditions in the Soviet żone. The measures adopted by the zonal rulers subject the people of central Germany to the severest possible pressure and place them in a situation of profound moral dilemma.

In view of this tragic fate of our compatriots beyond the zonal border, the Christian Democratic Union is encouraging and supporting every effort to achieve joint action in All-German affairs by all political forces. It is convinced that in the present position greater unanimity in the work devoted to reunification is an essential prerequisite in overcoming the partition of Germany.

OPPOSITION PARTY VIEWS [12]

The outer semblance of the third German Bundestag [parliament] creates the impression of greater simplicity on the German political scene. Only four or rather three and a half parties are now represented in the Bundestag and the government party has a clear numerical advantage over the Social Democrats who constitute the largest party in opposition.

The third Adenauer government, . . . however, was hard in the making. The explanation for this is to be found in the conflicts among the interest groups who have now found their home in the Christian Democratic party. . . . The toughness of these conflicts has led even the Chancellor to complain about the undue pressure of the interest groups. He should be the last one to be surprised however, since he must realize better than anyone that the interest groups would present their bill, after the elections, for the heavy monetary contributions with which they helped the Christian Democrats finance their campaign.

The dangers inherent to the democratic process, inherent in these methods of financing an election, are so obvious that it should be one of the first tasks of the Bundestag to pass a law which will bring the financing of political parties under effective public control.

We also warn the majority of this House of any further manipulation of the electoral laws. It would perhaps be best to

12 From "The Tasks of the Third Bundestag," speech by Erich Ollenhauer, chairman of the West German Social Democratic Party. *News From Germany* (published by the executive committee of the Social Democratic party of Germany). 11:1-3. December 1957.

embody the electoral system in the Basic Law (Constitution) and remove it thereby from the tactical considerations of a party. . . .

One should respect the proper function of the parliamentary opposition during the campaign, as well. The Federal Chancellor went so far in his allegations and slander during the campaign as to depict the Social Democratic party as the veritable enemy of the state. Political differences and disagreements are essential to the democratic process, but to keep our democracy vital we need at least a minimum of respect for the political opponent and a minimum of trust in his loyalty to the constitutional order. This we missed.

I want to repeat, however, that the Social Democratic party has always been and still is prepared to cooperate with the government in questions that are vital to the nation. But this is possible only if the government is also prepared to furnish the opposition with the information to which the government party has hitherto had sole access. It is just as necessary that the government inform the opposition about its intentions before making a fundamental decision, in order to give the latter a chance to deliberate on what may be accepted and what must be rejected in such a decision.

The method of first making a decision and then asking the opposition whether they are in agreement with this decision, which has hitherto been employed by the government, is completely out of the question. The Social Democrats shall never be prepared to accept the position of a satellite. . . . The Social Democratic party represents the votes of nine and one half million German voters, and we regard it as our solemn duty to preserve and strengthen the confidence of these voters. Consequently we do not regard our work as done when we simply negate the position of the government, but shall make every effort to guide the work of parliament according to our own concepts of the inner and outer order of our affairs.

The solution of these problems begins with the shaping of our internal policies, in the proper sense of this word. Parliamentary democracy cannot be limited. We are not altogether free from worry in this respect and fear that certain authoritarian tendencies on the part of the government will only be strengthened in the future. Our fears are based on the experience of the recent campaign, as well. The extent to which a fusion of party and state has taken place, witnessed by the use of public facilities on the part of the Christian Democratic parties (CDU/CSU), is no longer in agreement with the democratic principle of division between party and state.

From time to time we have demanded that the secret funds of which the Federal Chancellor disposes should be placed under parliamentary control. We have also opposed the use of auxiliary organizations such as the "Working Committee of Democratic Circles" (Arbeitsgemeinschaft Demokratischer Kreise), who supported by public means supply the government with a one-sided propaganda channel. These methods of influencing public opinion are unbearable and we shall ask parliament to decide on a change during the next budget debate.

The support of scientific endeavor deserves special mention. This is one of the decisive political problems, today. We must sponsor technology and scientific research in such a way that they will be used to improve man's welfare instead of further enslaving him. We must provide our students with a solid financial basis, and expand our present school system so as to be able to offer the best in knowledge and education for character and citizenship to them. The crass differences between the much praised economic miracle and the condition of science constitutes one of the most serious challenges to the policies of the government and its coalition partners.

The Protection of the Populace

Our membership in NATO and the existence of the Bundeswehr [army] are part of the pressing problems which also belong in the realm of internal policy. The development of the intercontinental ballistic missiles has forced the world powers to reevaluate their conceptions of security measures to the new situation. . . . Only by carefully observing the developments among the world powers can the European states fit their own security measures to the new situation. If we are to be realistic in our judgment of this development we should also revamp our ideas about the mandatory security measures. The federal government is responsible in this case for informing the people about what will be done to protect their health and life in case of a conflict.

It is lamentable that the same government which allows atomic stockpiles on German territory has not found the time to inform the German people of the consequences of atomic war and about what can and must be done for the populace. The modern weapons make a thorough study of their effects and possible protective measures absolutely mandatory. Only a commission of experts who are independent of the political and financial desires of the government, are capable of finding the facts. Such a commission should immediately be set up in order to enable parliament and government to draw the consequences from its findings.

The federal government is able to meet its military obligations through a force of volunteers—without having to resort to draft. The Social Democrats are still convinced that the general draft will deepen the German schism, harm us politically and is actually out of date from the military point of view. A certain number of tasks, however, are not fitted for the volunteer forces, which are to be placed under the command of an ally. We ask the federal government how it intends to fulfill these tasks which have expressly been placed into the category of territorial defense by national forces in several treaties.

The defense budget of 9 billion Deutsche Marks per annum will grow considerably, judging from the demands of the Ministry of Defense. This alone proves the declarations of the federal finance minister that the defense costs will not exceed 9 billion Deutsche Marks are not true. It is also clear that the armament orders and the new military quotas in the budget will exceed the capacity of the German economy. This means a reduction of social services while a new tax burden threatens us and the buying power of our money will sink further. In a word: the extent of defense spending is threatening the stability of our currency.

If one really intends to organize the security of the West German populace, without exceeding its financial capacity, one should establish an exact system of priorities. The federal government should explain in the Atlantic Council that the German populace, which lies directly next to the power orbit of the Soviets, deserves special attention in terms of its security. The government must for this reason oppose the foreign demands to speed up the establishment of the Bundeswehr so that it may relieve their own forces. Nor must military measures be allowed to shake our social foundations and at the same time endanger our not too solid democracy. This will only be possible if the protection of the populace and home defense have been properly organized, and the operative forces under NATO command been limited to what is absolutely necessary.

DEBATE ON ATOMIC ARMS [13]

On July 6 [1958], the elections for the regional Parliament of the Landtag were held in North Rhine-Westphalia. The outcome was a complete victory for the Christian Democratic Union, Chancellor Adenauer's party, which won an absolute majority of votes in this Land for the first time and so was put in a position to replace the coalition government of the Social Democrats and Free Democrats with a straight CDU government. North Rhine-Westphalia is the most important Land in the Federal Republic with regard to population and economic resources; in its center, along the Rhine and Ruhr, lies the industrial region that is the chief Social Democrat stronghold. But it is not for this reason alone that the regional elections and their result were so important. In fighting the election battle, both the CDU and the SPD [Social Democrats] largely ignored the true and indigenous issues involved and concentrated almost exclusively on Bonn's external and internal policies. . . .

The Last Bundestag Elections

The campaign in North Rhine-Westphalia undoubtedly represents the most critical phase of the CDU's struggle to defend the basis of its foreign policy. . . . Last fall it was pos-

[13] From " 'Atomic Death' in Western Germany," article by Fred Luchsinger, foreign correspondent of the *Neue Zürcher Zeitung* in Bonn. *Swiss Review of World Affairs.* 8:6-8. August 1958. Reprinted by permission.

sible to have a reasonable doubt as to whether Chancellor
Adenauer's national victory of September 15 really did represent
the German people's vote of confidence for the foreign policy
pursued up till then. The prosperity of that time and the wish
to continue the economic policies ensuring it might have been
at least as decisive. . . .

The opposition tried to establish a balance by giving the
people an apocalyptic version of atomic war, thereby hoping
to show that the policy regarding security is an illusion. Chancellor Adenauer, who has never allowed the opposition to determine his platform and in any case prefers to take the offensive,
wisely avoided the atomic subject, in order to keep the voters
from becoming uncertain of the security he promised them. He
retired behind his own politically rather prematurely given hints
of an atomic armament, announcing that this question was not
of immediate interest.

The Atomic Threat in Politics

Shortly after election day, however, it became just this. . . .
Chancellor Adenauer and his party openly declared themselves
in favor of the army's atomic armament and, though put at a
disadvantage by this, had to face the public whether they liked
to or not. After the parliamentary battle in Bonn, the outcome
of which was, of course, guaranteed by the majority situation,
many a politician in the government camp began to be seriously
worried about the future success of the trump card "security"
under these circumstances.

Convinced that at long last they had also gained the upper
hand in regard to foreign policy and that they could now deal
Chancellor Adenauer's policy a crippling blow, the opposition
set to work on the mobilization of the masses. The idea was
that anxiety, fear and uneasiness would overcome the lethargy
of the well-fed German citizen and the desire for security would
no longer uphold the previous policy of security, but quite to
the contrary, stand in its way. . . .

A French observer, surprised by the "immobility" of the
German voter and his disinclination to let himself be impressed

by such immense facts as those of atomic development, has asked the question, whether in German elections a choice is still made for a certain policy, or whether it is not rather a matter of blindly giving a vote of confidence to a political leader because of his personality. The question cannot be taken lightly, and it also cannot be answered in the negative for a part of the electorate. Nevertheless, the fact remains that besides Chancellor Adenauer's unshaken authority a great number of other reasons combined to cause the failure of the anti-atomic campaign.

A few of these reasons are provided by the opponents of atomic armament themselves. They fought "against atomic death"; but they did not succeed in making the public believe that those in favor of atomic armament were also "for atomic death." In reality the differences of opinion on this question represented the efforts made on both sides to find the best method of preventing an atomic war. Seen from this objective viewpoint, it must be admitted that the advocates of atomic armament at least acted in good faith, and that a number of their arguments must be considered valid—which in turn makes it difficult in the long run to continue the debate on an entirely emotional level.

At a second glance it also appears doubtful whether Germany's exclusion from atomic armament would offer it the greatest amount of protection against an atomic war. This was the naïve thesis of the Göttingen professors' manifesto one and a half years ago. The well-known physicist von Weizsäcker, its initiator, has in the meantime revised much of it for his own personal satisfaction, after its effect on the public had already begun to wear off. During his visit in Bonn, A. I. Mikoyan attempted to bolster the theory with his assurances that the Soviet Union would certainly not launch an atomic attack on a country that has barred all nuclear weapons from its territory. Characteristically enough, the opposition has made little use of his statement; in Germany it is impossible to base propaganda on a Soviet promise. The thesis was whittled down to the one declaration, that the absence of atomic weapons at least decreases the danger—even though this cannot be eliminated entirely.

The American Presence

An especially weak and vulnerable link in the chain of anti-atomic arguments was the question of the presence of the Americans in Europe and the Federal Republic in particular. Had the Germans demanded that their greatest ally stop preparing for an atomic defense that would make up for the inferiority in troops and conventional fire-power, they would have then run the risk of an American withdrawal not only from their country but also from the European Continent as such. It is, of course, true that in order to avoid being accused of interfering in Germany's internal affairs, Washington has never issued a top level declaration to this effect; but the possibility of such a . . . solution was nevertheless distinct enough, and weighed heavily against the opponents of atomic armament. . . .

Disturbance of the Peace

From the beginning, the complex nature of the whole problem implied that the campaign against atomic armament would be short-lived. . . .

Hundreds of thousands joined the first campaign demonstrations of protest but soon their ranks had thinned out considerably. . . .

In addition there were also several adverse influences that came from the outside. The execution of Imre Nagy and his associates was a particularly heavy blow the Soviets dealt themselves; it again destroyed that minimum of trust requisite to any policy of disengagement and any agreement on armament. . . .

What Was the Use?

The campaign against atomic armament has not been called off, . . . but it has lost its vigor. . . . It is more than likely that the whole theme will gradually be forced out of party politics altogether and will so fade from view as a politically formative factor in the Federal Republic.

III. EAST GERMANY—COMMUNIST RULE

EDITOR'S INTRODUCTION

East Germany is now ruled as one of the Soviet satellites of Eastern Europe with a score or more Russian military divisions stationed on its soil. East of the Soviet zone are still other former German territories, now controlled by Poland and the Soviet Union. A significant portion of pre-World War II eastern Germany is now under Polish administration and the are set forth by a newspaper correspondent from Berlin, Arthur istration between Poland and the U.S.S.R. (see map, p. 10). Of these territories little is now heard in the debate about re-unifying 'Germany. Nor do the following articles deal with them specifically.

The basic facts about East Germany—the German Democratic Republic—and the tenor of life under Communist rule are set forth by the newspaper correspondent from Berlin, Arthur J. Olsen. The importance the Soviet bloc attaches to its most western outpost in Europe is noted in an *Atlantic Monthly* report. And the recent economic goals which the Communist regime has announced are spelled out in a dispatch by Sydney Gruson.

As in West Germany, the problems of former Nazis and today's refugees also plague East Germany, though in entirely different ways, as indicated in the next two articles. The first, by another correspondent from Berlin, indicates that the East German government is perhaps embarrassed but not really concerned about the number of former Nazi officials now in office.

The West German government statement about the refugees gives an insight into conditions now imposed by the East German dictatorship. Further facts about legal and other restrictions under which the East Germans live are indicated in the significant report which was presented to the Council of Europe in October 1958. A New York *Herald Tribune* article suggests that the rulers of East Germany have returned to ancient practices in following Moscow dictates about education-plus-work schemes.

The two articles which follow present a somewhat different view of the status of East Germany from what might be gathered from either West German sources or other articles in this book. The articles from a special correspondent for the *Economist*, the influential British journal, suggest that the East German regime, like West Germany, is undergoing a significant economic revival, despite earlier, sometimes Soviet-inspired, obstacles, and may well become a permanent state which may not for the foreseeable future be reunited with West Germany.

That Moscow would like to solidify Communist power in East Germany is noted in the last article; it raises also larger questions about Germany as a whole which are dealt with more fully in the next section.

GERMANS UNDER COMMUNISM [1]

A nation, by minimum definition, is an extension of inhabited territory presided over by a government capable of asserting its authority over the land and people.

At this rudimentary level the German Democratic Republic, a territory in north central Europe extending over 46,600 square miles and inhabited by 17 million German-speaking people, is indeed a state.

At a more sophisticated level the East German Republic hardly qualifies. Nine years after its formal birth it remains essentially the zone occupied by the Soviet Union in consequence of the arbitrary parceling up of defeated Germany at the close of World War II.

The Soviet zone comprises the five old German provinces of Mecklenburg, Brandenburg, Sachsen-Anhalt, Saxony and Thuringia, plus a part of Pomerania. This area taken as a unit has played no special role in German history. Neither does it constitute a plausible geographic or economic unit.

[1] From "East Germany Ruled by an Ersatz Regime," by Arthur J. Olsen, correspondent. New York *Times*. p E4. December 7, 1958. Reprinted by permission.

The inhabitants of the German Democratic Republic, which is about as big as New York State, have hardly more "national" consciousness as Middle Germans or East Germans than do New Yorkers as New Yorkers.

Every genuine nation has a recognized capital and in East Germany this could only be the mighty cosmopolitan city of Berlin. But the German Democratic Republic is governed from only the one third of Berlin under Soviet occupation and specifically from the Borough of Pankow. The United States Government would be in the same position if it disposed only of the northwest district of Washington, the remainder of the capital being occupied by a hostile population and foreign military forces.

To overcome this crushing psychological handicap is one of the main reasons why the East German authorities are thirsting to end the four-power occupation of Berlin and eventually to run the Western Allies out of the city.

Another quality of genuine nationhood is freedom from foreign control. The German Democratic Republic, according to its constitution and its claims, is sovereign. In fact, however, it is a fief of Moscow run by a German Communist dictator named Walter Ulbricht.

As chairman of the Communist party and deputy premier Herr Ulbricht directs an elaborate machinery of government patterned along the authoritarian lines of the Communist "people's democracies."

Soviet Force

Yet it is a fair guess that the whole structure would come apart in a few weeks but for the presence of twenty-two Soviet army divisions on the sovereign territory of the East German Republic. The Ulbricht regime did in fact collapse for a few hours on June 17, 1953, when tens of thousands of East Germans revolted against a work speedup decree. Soviet tanks and troops poured out of the barracks they inconspicuously inhabit and restored order at the price of a few thousand German lives.

Superficially the East German state looks more like a representative democracy, than does the average "people's democracy."

This is due to a situation in the early postwar years when the occupation zones were thought to be temporary administrative units and the Germans took at face value the Potsdam pledge to revive democratic political life throughout Germany.

As late as 1948 the Communist-approved candidates could attract the votes of only 60 per cent of the Soviet-zone residents. This was long after the purge of bourgeois politicians had eliminated anti-Communist leadership and political terror had been instituted.

The Pankow regime is a party dictatorship of the Socialist Unity party, the product of forced marriage in 1946 between the Communist and Socialist parties. Under the 1949 constitution veteran Communist leader Wilhelm Pieck became president of the republic. A fellow-traveling Socialist, Otto Grotewohl, was named premier and still holds the job.

Aged, infirm Pieck is a figurehead. So is Grotewohl, although he is responsible for the routine administration of government. The boss is Ulbricht, a hard lifelong Communist who was sent out from Moscow by Stalin in 1945 to organize the civil administration of the Soviet zone.

Moscow's Man

Moscow has never had any "revisionist" troubles with Ulbricht. He travels often to the Soviet capital for policy discussions.

The Soviet military administration was converted into the Soviet Control Commission in 1949 upon the establishment of civilian government. On March 27, 1954, the Soviets declared the German Democratic Republic "sovereign" and abolished its formal agency of control. But a Soviet general still resides in East Berlin.

According to the 1949 constitution the highest organ of state is the Volkskammer or Parliament. Its 400 members are elected from a single list prepared before quadrennial elections. The Socialist Unity party is assigned 100 seats and four other parties, non-Communist but docile, have forty-five each. The remaining 120 seats are assigned to the Communist-run "mass organizations," notably the trade union federation and the "Free German Youth." Thus, in the unlikely event of a bourgeois party revolt in the Volkskammer, Ulbricht would command a solid majority, with 220 votes.

The Soviet zone regime has had two highly important tasks to fulfill for the Soviet Union. The first was to root a Communist society firmly in the heart of Germany. The second was to provide an industrial arsenal for the rest of the Soviet bloc, which is still short of such highly-developed people as the Germans.

On balance Ulbricht has made some progress on the first assignment but hardly enough from Moscow's standpoint. No one knows how many East Germans would vote Communist in a free election. But Western analysts stand by their long-standing estimate of less than 10 per cent.

Soviet zone residents are still fleeing through the West Berlin escape hatch at the rate of four or five thousand a week. In the last few months this open wound has hurt Pankow more than ever because the proportion of well-treated intellectuals and technicians has increased in the refugee movement.

Despite its failure to win over the hearts of the people, Pankow plows ahead ruthlessly at the job of "building socialism." The private share of the national product has gone down from 41 per cent in 1950 to 26 per cent last year.

Pankow has done much better in its role as manufacturer and artisan in the service of the Communist community.

War Loot

In the first place it enriched the Soviet Union during the first eight postwar years with some $12 billion in cash and kind exacted by means of factory dismantling, forced payments, profits of Soviet-run East German firms and give-away prices of East German goods shipped to the East.

The outright looting has ended. Instead the Soviet Union is putting capital into East German industry so that it may better fulfill its assigned role as the fabricator of Communist bloc raw materials into finished goods for reexport.

The Soviet zone could never become self-supporting and its industrial plant is shabby by Western standards. But in the "common market" the Soviet Union has fashioned out of its satellites, East Germany is a star performer and a highly important member.

RUSSIA'S INTEREST IN EAST GERMANY [2]

Keystone of the Soviet Bloc?

It has sometimes been supposed that East Germany might, sooner or later, become too much of a burden to the Soviet Union. Federal Chancellor Konrad Adenauer, for instance, believes this, and as late as last summer [1957] West German newspapers were publishing reports of approaching political revolution and economic catastrophe in East Germany.

But recent developments suggest that, far from becoming a burden, East Germany is to an increasing extent becoming the keystone of the satellite bloc and of Soviet policies in central Europe. Last January an agreement was signed defining the status of Soviet troops in Germany and making them liable for trial in German courts for civil offenses. In June [1957] Polish Prime Minister Wladislaw Gomulka visited East Berlin at the insistence of Nikita Khrushchev. He signed a trade agreement with East German Prime Minister Otto Grotewohl, promised full cooperation between the two countries, and confirmed the permanence of the Oder-Neisse Line as Germany's eastern frontier.

On August 7 Khrushchev himself came to Berlin and spoke in the East German Parliament. He gave his full support to the Grotewohl Plan for the creation of a German Confederation, in which both German states would retain their own administrations, laws, and economic setups. The Grotewohl Plan laid down three conditions for the formation of the confederation: phased withdrawal of the armed forces of the great powers from Germany, a ban on the production and storing of nuclear

[2] From "The Atlantic Report on the World Today—Berlin." *Atlantic Monthly*. 201:6+. January 1958. Reprinted by permission.

weapons on German soil, and the withdrawal of West Germany from NATO. Khrushchev backed the plan and repeated the now standard Soviet demand for all-German talks as the necessary preliminary to German reunification.

The Kremlin Puts on the Heat

On September 20 [1957] the Soviet Union formally recognized the absolute sovereignty of the East German Republic. This step suggests that German reunification, on any terms, has been written off in Moscow. It was only natural that Khrushchev should then have put pressure to bear on Marshal Tito to recognize the East German Republic. Yugoslavia did this on October 14, and a few days later the Federal Republic reluctantly found itself forced to break off diplomatic relations with Yugoslavia.

Full of high hopes, East German trade missions have since gone to Egypt, India, and Syria, seeking recognition of the East German Republic by countries outside the Communist bloc.

It is always possible for the Soviet Union to organize events in the interests of a puppet state. It is less easy for the Soviet Union, thus far, to ensure that puppet's material progress. East Germany has suffered more than any other satellite from Communist economic rule—from the drift of skilled labor to the more attractive West German market, from exploitation of its most valuable resources, from the contradictions of economic despotism and an enduring lack of real patriotism. East Germany's population is actually declining. For instance, that of two of its few big cities, Dresden and Chemnitz, has fallen by 13,000 and 8,000 respectively in the last four years. Would it not, therefore, be reasonable to expect its economy to decline too? That, at any rate, is one of Konrad Adenauer's hopes.

To a great extent East Germany's continued existence as a state will depend on its economic viability. The Soviet Union would not welcome, and might even have to discard, the dead weight of an economically bankrupt East Germany. But the economic value of a prosperous East Germany to the Communist bloc is considerable.

The East German is still conditioned to austerity. He can buy a liter of milk for each of his children at a cut rate of 25 pfennigs, or 6 cents. But the three liters a head which he must buy additionally cost 1.20 marks, or 28 cents, each. One pound of beef costs the equivalent of 40 cents on the ration, but $1.30 on the free market. The corresponding prices for butter are 50 cents and $1.70, and for sugar, 13 cents and 36 cents. And the basic rations for meat, fat, and sugar are only 2.7, 1.8, and 2.4 pounds a month. Free market prices, like those of 60 cents for a half liter of Pilsener lager and $2.50 for a square meal at a restaurant, are out of line with industrial workers' average wages of only $100 to $120 a month.

At the Munich October Festival, the traditional fare is chicken roasted on the spit, washed down by the best beer in Europe. At the People's Festivals in East Germany, it is waste-meat sausages and pea soup. The beer is thin, chemical stuff. The East German is equally conditioned to poor clothing, bad footwear, and a chronic housing shortage. A quarter of a million homes have been built in the last ten years; in West Germany half a million are built each year. The Federal Republic has forty-one automobiles to every thousand inhabitants; East Germany has five.

Plugging the Holes

Stringencies have not prevented the steady stabilization of the East German economy. In October 1956, paper currency was called in, and as a result the value of notes in circulation has been reduced from 5.8 billion to around 4.7 billion marks. Last spring a thousand utility shops were used to run off surplus stocks of cheap stuff, and the introduction of installment buying has brought sales worth another one billion marks. The gap caused by reduced deliveries of Polish coal was plugged with Russian imports from the Donetz basin.

Since the Hungarian Revolution [in 1956], imports of Russian rolled steel products have also been substantially increased. Walter Ulbricht has promised that East Germany will be almost self-supporting in foodstuffs by the last year of the present Five Year Plan—1960—and he has said that he will try to abolish food rationing next year as well. Already the rationing system is due less to shortages than to the difficulty of abolishing a dual pricing system which gives some minimal protection to the lowest income groups. . . .

Limited industrial failures can always be made good by the Soviet Union, as happened during 1957. In return, East Germany will go on producing large quantities of uranium ore, chemicals, fertilizers, machinery, and precision instruments needed by the whole Communist bloc.

Political Control

The twenty-two Red Army divisions are being kept in East Germany for political, even more than for strictly military, reasons. The Hungarian revolution taught the Soviet leaders just how tenuous their hold was on the satellites. Their garrisons in East Germany discourage Poland from emulating Hungary's example and help to keep Czechoslovakia in its place. A strong, united Germany could be a rival focus and threat to Soviet predominance in central Europe.

That is why the Grotewohl-Ulbricht regime will be maintained in power, and why it is being helped in taking steps to ensure its survival.

ECONOMIC TARGETS [3]

The Soviet threats against Berlin are being accompanied by a booming propaganda campaign in East Germany to convince the people that the good life is just around the corner.

"Togetherness" is one of the major themes of the campaign. Together with the Soviet Union, the theme goes, the people and the government will make such a paradise of East Germany by 1961 that the bright lights of West Germany will fade into disfavor.

In a gamble that the aims of their economic drive can be fulfilled, the Russians are putting up fairly heavy stakes. They have already agreed to give East Germans the equivalent of

[3] From "Large Goals Set in East Germany," by Sydney Gruson, correspondent. New York *Times*. p E5. November 23, 1958. Reprinted by permission.

nearly $200 million in economic aid next year—more than half of it in freely convertible foreign exchange.

And more will be forthcoming, according to both East Germans and Russians. The East German Communists make no secret of what they want. It is to outstrip West Germany in per capita production of major consumer goods and at the same time make up for lost time by turning East Germany into a major industrial power of the Communist bloc, second only to the Soviet Union itself.

People Unenthusiastic

Most Western experts . . . believe that they will fail in the first objective for a variety of reasons, including lack of enthusiasm for the regime among the people and the lead already established by West Germany.

The East German authorities have so far used more carrot than stick in trying to persuade their people to fall in with the plans. There are not many measuring rods available in the West for judging the mood of the East German people. Except for the tightly controlled annual pilgrimage to the Leipzig Fair, Western reporters and diplomats have been barred from the region.

No one here takes seriously the results of [the election on November 16, 1958]. The Communists' National Front probably did get 99.87 per cent of the vote, as claimed, but that very unanimity spoiled whatever effect the election might have had here.

German thoroughness and Communist determination left very few persons with an opportunity to avoid an appearance at the polls. And the East Germans had long ago discounted the effectiveness of the dangerous gesture of voting against the single list of Communist candidates.

Perhaps a more revealing measure of the East Germans' contentment with their regime is the continuing flight to the West of 20,000 people monthly. The number of manual workers among the refugees has tapered off while the number of intellectuals and students among them has risen—indicating an easing of the pressures that led the workers to rise in revolt in 1953 and that kept them simmering afterward.

Industrial Gap

The size of the task facing the East German regime can be judged partly in a comparison of the industrial output of West Germany and East Germany. . . . [In 1957 steel production in West Germany stood at nearly 25 million metric tons; in East Germany at only 2.5 million. For the same year the West Germans produced 160 million metric tons of coal and East Germany less than half that figure, 75 million.—Ed.]

On consumer goods, the gap is even wider. West Germany, for example, produced in 1956 more than 1 million cars and trucks and the East Germans 33,000. On radio sets the figures were 3.2 million in West Germany and 650,000 in East Germany and on television sets 527,000 against 55,000.

Some of the targets the East Germans have set themselves for 1960 are: Hard coal, 3 million tons; brown coal, 300 million tons; iron and steel, 7.5 million tons; cars and motorized bicycles, 35,000 units; television sets, 270,000 units.

East Germany is the westernmost outpost of communism, the country best placed to be a showcase of Marxist planning and labor. Besides, it surrounds an island of free enterprise and capitalist endeavor—West Berlin, whose bright lights and well-being make it difficult to boast of Communist superiority.

To make the West less attractive and to soothe the East German people is certainly one reason for the economic drive. But for the Russians there is an equally compelling reason in Moscow's search for additional industrial resources to help its economic penetration of the underdeveloped areas of the world.

Skilled Workers

An industrial base and skilled workers are available in East Germany perhaps to a higher degree than in any other Communist country. These have been misused or not used at all up to now; and the Russians are reported to have been impressed finally by what the West achieved by investing in West German know-how and energy.

In effect the Russians are saying: the people of West Germany and of East Germany are the same. With similar investments, we can achieve similar results in East Germany.

But there is an intangible factor that Premier Khrushchev and Walter Ulbricht, East German Communist leader, cannot control. This is the extent of cooperation they will receive from East German workers.

Some subtlety has crept into the Communists' handling of the workers of East Germany. Trade union organization has become more flexible and more responsive to the workers' demands. Unlike 1953, when the screws were tightened on the industrial population, 1958 finds the Communists concerned with signs of unrest and adept recently at loosening controls to meet grumbling at its outset.

Western Allied experts here agree that, since the Hungarian revolution of 1956, a certain stability has been achieved in East Germany because the majority of its people see no alternative. All available figures show steadily rising production and there is no doubt that the people are living better than twelve or eighteen months ago.

That they can be brought up to the level of West Germany by 1961 is doubtful, in the opinion of Western economists. But the same experts concede that the East Germans can be brought a long way from their present level. Khrushchev and company are gambling that this will be enough to pay off the Soviet investment with profit.

USE OF NAZI OFFICIALS [4]

The Communist regime of East Germany is reported to be proceeding cautiously with a reduction of the number of former Nazis in positions of prominence in the government and in state industries and cultural institutions.

This process calls for delicate handling by the regime because it involves its propaganda position abroad and its efforts for unity at home.

[4] From "Ex-Nazi Officials Vex Red Germany," by Harry Gilroy, correspondent. New York *Times.* p25. August 24, 1958. Reprinted by permission.

For years the East German regime has asserted that the West German government is full of former members of the National Socialist party. The East Germans have ignored, in their effort to establish a propaganda point, the fact that many foes of Hitlerism have leading places in the Bonn Government.

In June [1958], an anti-Communist organization in West Berlin, the Investigation Committee of Free Jurists, made public a study of "brown spots" in East Germany.

This listed as former Nazis seventy-six persons of high rank in East Germany. The list had an air of authenticity because after each name there was given the number of the National Socialist party card held by the man, the date of its issuance and in many cases party distinctions that had been achieved.

The list purported to show that twenty-nine members of the Volkskammer, the East German legislature, were former Nazis. One of the deputy presidents of the Volkskammer was listed and such prominent officials as the minister of health and chairman of the Research Council of the Board of Ministers.

Leading editors of newspapers published by the Socialist Unity (Communist) party were included in the list of former Nazi party members. Professors heading East German colleges and directors of state-owned industries also were named.

All this took some of the force out of the East German propaganda against the "Fascist state in Bonn," as the slogan went. It may have been only coincidence, but East German leaders began to discuss publicly the problem of having too many former Nazis in government.

Deputy Premier Walter Ulbricht, who heads the Communist party apparatus in East Germany, mentioned this in his address to the Socialist Unity Party Congress in July. Among his listeners was Soviet Premier Nikita S. Khrushchev.

Herr Ulbricht observed that "bourgeois influence has considerably increased in the state apparatus." He cited as an example the council for the district of Erfurt, ninety miles southwest of Berlin.

"In the council," Herr Ulbricht said, "there are fifty-six former officers and sergeants of the Fascist Wehrmacht [army] and forty members of the Nazi party."

The party leader said that while he was not opposed to having former officers in government posts, he wanted "no concentration of former officers and members of the Nazi party."

Since this speech there have been reports that here and there employees with a Nazi past have been shifted to avoid the concentrations that Herr Ulbricht deprecated.

WHY THEY FLEE [5]

Contrary to frequent world-wide predictions, which even today occasionally find currency, the German people have never reconciled themselves to the perpetuation of the division of their country. . . .

It is a cause of the deepest distress to the federal Parliament, federal government and the German people that since the division of our country more than 3 million people have had to leave their homes in central Germany, and of whom no fewer than 2,123,610 submitted an application for recognition as bona fide refugees between January 1, 1949, and August 31, 1958. . . .

A National Catastrophe

Let me solemnly assure you on behalf of the federal government that we see in this migration of millions of people from that part of the Fatherland which is under Communist domination an utter fiasco of a regime that is so contrary to our tradition and outlook; but at the same time we are deeply concerned at the continuation of the "desertion" of the German Democratic Republic (DDR). The federal government does not desire, let alone promote, the bleeding of the already weakened population potential of central Germany. Far rather must the migration from this area be described as a national catastrophe. . . .

The flight of doctors is a particularly noticeable source of anxiety. It is evident that their flight, as that of other sections

[5] From "We Are One Nation and Wish to Remain So!" a West German government statement read to Parliament by Ernst Lemmer, Federal Minister for All-German Affairs. *The Bulletin* (issued by the Press and Information Office of the German Federal Government). 6:2+. October 7, 1958.

of the population, is a consequence of intensified Sovietization. The sober and yet so revealing figures are as follows:

From January 1, 1958, to August 31, 1958, 813 doctors, veterinarians and dentists, as against 260 in the same period last year, as well as 115 pharmacists compared with 33 in the previous year, have fled from central Germany to the Federal Republic. This flight has led to threatening conditions in certain important sectors of the public health service. Numerous localities and individual hospitals are temporarily without medical service. . . .

The federal government has never and at no time—and this must be repeated with all clarity—recruited or lent its hand to the recruitment of doctors from the Soviet-occupied zone, even though the Politburo of the SED [Socialist Unity party] has had the audacity to assert this time and time again. . . .

The flight of teaching and research staffs must be particularly embarrassing to the Communist authorities in East Berlin. Since the beginning of the year more than 250 professors, lecturers and academic assistants have left the Soviet-occupied zone. Not because they were materially badly off, not at all! They all emphasized that they were well paid, even more than well paid, and materially were exposed to no suffering. The one decisive cause of their flight is the "socialist reconstruction" of the universities, which the SED has pursued energetically since the beginning of the year. This socialization demands from professors, lecturers and assistants categorical and public acknowledgment of dialectical materialism. This is an acknowledgment that many are not in a position to make, since it is in their opinion simultaneously a public acknowledgment of atheism.

There is also a remarkable increase in the number of teachers fleeing, and this, too, is due to growing political pressure and divergence of outlook. In August alone, 619 teachers applied for refugee status. Of these, 412—more than two thirds—received their training after 1945. More than 2,300 teachers have fled since the beginning of the year. Since the larger part of the teachers have been in service a long time and are married, and since it is common knowledge in the zone that supplementary training lasting several semesters is demanded in the Federal area, it is clear how severe the conflict is which leads them to give up their professional existence. . . .

The responsibility for all this must be born by a government which has never as yet received a democratic legitimation for its measures from the people. Instead of subjecting themselves to a critical examination in light of the hostile attitude of all sections of the population—whether workers, farmers, the intelligentsia, middle-class people, or even functionaries of the party, state and industry—they have sought to prevent "desertion of the republic" with inhuman means.

Searches, barriers, checks, confiscation, propaganda and severe punishment are the means which are in daily use. Of the measures which have caused the greatest unrest among the population of the Soviet zone can be primarily mentioned the Amendment to the Passport Law issued on December 11, 1957. According to this, journeys within Germany are treated as foreign travel. They have to be approved and every non-observance of the regulations is liable to punishment.

Further repressions result from the newly introduced "German Democratic Republic [DDR] citizenship." Whereas the Soviet zone constitution still states expressly in Article 1, Paragraph 4, that there is only one German citizenship, now in a mere administrative order, reference is made to "citizenship of the German Democratic Republic." This occurs without any change having been made in the DDR Constitution violated thereby.

It is a consequence of this alleged citizenship of the DDR that former "deserters of the republic" who, for example, visit the Soviet zone after many years of residence in the Federal Republic are arrested, deprived of their Federal German identification card, punished and finally prevented from returning to the Federal Republic and in this way compelled by force to remain in the Soviet zone.

With the same argument of the "citizenship of the DDR," children of parents who are "deserters of the republic" are prevented from joining their families or their parents in the event of their returning to the DDR. The parents are not only kept apart from their children, but they are formally deprived of the rights of care and protection in that these children become the "wards of the DDR" contrary to the wishes of the parents. . . .

This description of the situation of our fellow countrymen in central Germany reveals the utter misery of the present German lot. In this connection, it should not remain unremarked that the spiritual and intellectual attitude of the population under the unceasing blows of the ideological hammer of the SED seems simply admirable. I reject most emphatically the widespread pessimism in the West concerning the inner bearing of our countrymen in the zone. If the revolt of June 1953 attracted the attention of the world, so today must their quiet, sensible and controlled behavior be regarded with the deepest respect. The brutal attempt of the Ulbricht regime to destroy the unity of our people through the denial of freedom of movement within our common homeland is condemned to failure. Of that the federal government is convinced. . . .

The Efforts of the Federal Government

It is of the utmost importance to the federal government in the present moment to relieve, and where possible eliminate, the human suffering which results from inhuman measures and affects hundreds of thousands on that side and this side of the zonal border.

The federal government, as previously, will support all discussions of a technical nature between the competent authorities, in so far as such discussions are likely to bring about an improvement in the situation of the population. On the basis of previous experience, however, the possibilities of this are unfortunately slight, as the Soviet zone authorities, as already emphasized, pursue political ends first of all, and these indeed without reference to the situation of the population. The Soviet zone counter-proposals—for example, the setting up of a commission consisting of representatives from both sides and empowered to deal with problems affecting both parts of Germany—have hitherto all had one aim: the recognition of the government of the Soviet zone, which has never received the legal sanction of the population. The federal government and, I am convinced, this Parliament as well are not prepared, any more than ever, to grant recognition of this kind. . . .

In this connection the point must be made that we consider it as a matter of course that with reunification the present form of the Federal Republic will be open to discussion in a freely elected All-German Parliament. There can be no question of the federal government attempting what would be the incorporation of central Germany. There will be no policy of reprisals against the SED, when ultimately the national unity of our people has been restored. . . .

Appeal to the Soviet Union

The continuing flight of refugees, the restriction on travel, the fortification of the zonal boundary and the far-reaching prevention of all personal contact within Germany by the Soviet zone authorities, as I have just described, are condemned throughout the world. This cannot be unknown to the Soviet government either. The federal government once again and without respite will use direct and appropriate channels to draw the attention of the Soviet government to the severe strain on German-Soviet relations resulting from the serious situation of the 17 million Germans in the DDR.

The federal government and, I am convinced, all the parliamentary parties are sincere in their desire for an improvement in relations with the Soviet Union. But this improvement which we seek, depends decisively upon the situation of the people in central Germany. For we are, after all, responsible for one another. We are one nation and wish to remain so. We hope that the Soviet government will not continue to shut its eyes to this fact. Too much is dependent on this for both peoples.

We demand the observance of the basic rights of the citizens, as they are laid down even in the Constitution of the DDR. We demand free travel within the whole of Germany. We demand simply human treatment for 17 million Germans.

A LIFE RESTRICTED [6]

For the past year and more all the armed bodies of the [Soviet] zone have been devoting their main attention to military exercises in the form of street and house-to-house fighting, as well as surprise night operations by armored units. The military authorities are making an all-out effort, through newspapers and technical journals, to popularize the revolutionary fighting tradition of the Communists in the armed groups and to convert it into tactical training. Students and pupils of technical schools are forced to take part in military study courses.

What They Call "Justice"

The regime of fear is most clearly seen in the field of justice. Laws do not serve to uphold the right but are a means towards supporting and expanding Communist power. In March 1956 there appeared to be some tendency in Soviet zone legal circles towards upholding the principle of a state based on the rule of law. A "commission to review the code of criminal procedure" was formed in the Ministry of Justice and prepared a report containing practical proposals for amending or supplementing the code. Had they been adopted, the position of the accused before the Soviet zone criminal courts would have been considerably improved. But the thirtieth and thirty-third General Assemblies of the SED quashed these proposals. They were condemned as "liberalization trends" and rejected outright. Shortly afterwards the Criminal Law and the Passport Laws Act were promulgated, and the hunt was on.

Under the significant clause, "any person who attempts to overthrow the constitutional order of state and society in the German Democratic Republic by force or systematic subversion" is punishable as a traitor by not less than five years penal servitude and the seizure of his property. In serious cases the death penalty or penal servitude for life may be ordered. No attempt is made in all this to define the "constitutional order of the

⁶ From "A Briton Reports," report submitted to the Council of Europe by Peter Kirk, Conservative Member of the British Parliament. *The Bulletin* (issued by the Press and Information Office of the German Federal Government). 6:4-5. November 4, 1958.

German Democratic Republic." For example, one man was convicted of high treason because he deviated from the SED party line and sought his own road to socialism.

The Leipzig District Court found that the import and distribution of literature published by Jehovah's Witnesses were "treasonable propaganda and provocation" within the meaning of the law and sentenced two accused on 11 February 1958 to three and a half and two years' penal servitude.

The Chemnitz District Court sentenced a Soviet zone inhabitant to one and a half year's imprisonment because he had yielded to a request from some West German friends to supply them with a maidservant from his home town. He was found guilty of "inciting a young person to leave the Democratic Republic." There have been hundreds of similar cases. For example, two youths of fifteen and sixteen recently received heavy prison sentences for having visited the Federal Republic.

"Socialization" of Agriculture

Measures to "socialize" farms have been taken since the start of the Soviet occupation of central Germany. The first step was expropriation (without compensation) of all farms with over 100 hectares (247 acres) of productive land—the agrarian reform of 1945 and 1946. The second step was the introduction of the agricultural producer cooperatives (LPG) in 1952. This was foreshadowed from 1949 onwards by ruthless propaganda against large farmers, in order to stir up public opinion against them as exploiting capitalists. The economic weapons used were, and still are, oppression through excessively high crop targets, unfavorable treatment in regard to allocations, of seeds, fertilizers, labor and machines on loan. (A large farmer, in Soviet zone terminology, is one whose total productive land exceeds 20 hectares [49 acres]. Owners of farms up to 20 hectares, and they alone, are known as working class farmers.)

Results of the system: in 1953, or more exactly up to the popular rising of 17 June, almost 14 per cent of the productive agricultural land has been transferred from private ownership to the LPG.

The new drive began about the beginning of this year. In the first quarter of 1958 productive farm land held by the LPG increased by about 3 per cent. This equals the increase in the whole of 1957. If the rate is maintained it will inevitably mean that by the end of 1958 at least 35 per cent, and by the end of 1960 at least 55 per cent, of the productive farm land will have been transferred from private ownership to the LPG. The feeling among independent farmers in the Soviet zone at present is one of despair.

Fight Against the Churches

The increased political pressure can also be felt in all aspects of cultural life. This is especially true of the churches, universities and schools, but it also applies, for example, to sport. The general trend is towards stifling or restricting all contacts and imposing an active and positive faith in dialectical and historical materialism.

The attack on the church, particularly the Evangelical Church, still occupies a special place in the general offensive. Furthermore, a major attempt is in progress to split the churches in order to break the resistance they have offered and still offer. The evident aim is an East-West schism, but at the same time a division within the Eastern church itself.

Under a new order dated 12 February 1958, the Christian teaching of the church is to be subordinated to state school supervision by atheist inspectors.

The struggle for man's soul reaches its climax in the growing pressures imposed upon the teachers themselves, culminating in the formula "a Christian cannot be a teacher." Hitherto it was possible to assert oneself as a positive Christian within the school sphere. Not so in future—opposition will henceforth be met by exclusion from the Party, and in almost all cases the result is ostracism.

University Opposition

Everywhere the indoctrination courses are being restarted for the intelligentsia, who are being ordered to "adopt" the fundamentals of historical and dialectical materialism. This means not only becoming acquainted with them, as before, but making them part and parcel of one's being.

This state of affairs is clearly bound to meet with some reaction. An interesting example is the Intellectuals' Conference at Halle on 12 April 1958. Here there was a genuine outbreak of opposition, and the Soviet zone party leaders attached so much importance to it that they printed a reply by the boldest of the audience, Professor Mothes (president of the Leopoldina [research institution], Halle) almost verbatim.

According to a Soviet zone newspaper, Professor Mothes said:

We need professors who have the courage sometimes to go their own way. I often wonder whether, in the conditions prevailing in universities today, men like Karl Marx and Engels would be given a hearing. They used to have violent arguments. Today, on every problem, other people always know better. A form of scholasticism is spreading that is inimical to all scientific development. . . . Professors live in constant disquiet. You must pardon me, Mr. Prime Minister, for frankly saying so. It is a fact. Some fundamental changes must be made.

Conclusion

The situation in the Soviet zone of Germany is becoming increasingly serious. The best proof of this is the growing number of refugees, many of them being people, who, as intellectuals, have enjoyed satisfactory material conditions in the Eastern zone. The root of the matter is thus manifestly the progressive suppression of human rights and fundamental freedoms, and the situation is one which concerns no longer Germany or Europe alone, but the whole of mankind.

A NEW FEUDALISM [7]

One of the most detested of feudal obligations was the *corvée.* This was the forced labor which the peasant owed his suzerain— so many days a year abstracted from working his own fields to till the lands of the lord of the manor. East Germany, under the modern tyranny of Marxism, is experiencing the revival of the *corvée,* and is resenting it, bitterly.

About eight weeks ago the East German Communist regime put into effect a pet idea of Nikita Khrushchev's, called, eu-

[7] From "Red 'Corvee' In East Germany," editorial. New York *Herald Tribune.* Section 2. p4. November 2, 1958. Reprinted by permission.

phemistically, "polytechnic education." In theory this was to be a kind of on-the-job training for school children from thirteen to eighteen years of age. In fact it meant the drafting of these children for one unpaid day a week to farms and factories. It was, in a word, the *corvée*.

The results have been bad. Teachers are complaining of the disruption of academic schedules and lowering of standards, factory managers say this undigested influx of untrained workers upsets routine and lowers production, parents charge that their children have been injured. "Several sixteen-year-old girls were blinded," said one mother in a public meeting in East Berlin, "after several hours of welding because there were not enough goggles to go around."

The practical instruction which the students are receiving does not counterbalance the losses imposed by the system. A factory inspector found only one of seven factories doing a good job in that respect, and an efficiency expert explained that "many of our production leaders and workers are not capable of instructing children." The same is true on the farms, where, according to the East German press, many children are simply set to shoveling manure, instead of being taught anything about agriculture.

The leader of East Germany's Communists, Walter Ulbricht, has been noted for following slavishly in the lead of any authority ruling the Kremlin. By being the first to give Khrushchev's "polytechnic education" a nation-wide trial, Ulbricht may have acquired merit with his Russian master. But he has also given the East Germans a taste of a regime which is worse than that of the medieval Junkers who were feudal lords of the soil centuries ago. The cause of freedom has thus actually been served by the new slave-drivers.

A LOOK OF PERMANENCE [8]

An extensive tour of East Germany [in the] spring [of 1958] can lead to no other conclusion than that the East German state is not going to collapse. Time is not on the Western side;

[8] From article by a special correspondent. *The Economist.* 187:125-6. April 12, 1958. Reprinted by permission.

indeed, the visitor is forced to doubt whether time is on the side of peace in central Europe if the present Eastern and Western policies are continued. Neither the Western taboo, nor the economic and psychological warfare conducted from Bonn, nor its own inherent weaknesses—not even the skepticism and hostility of a large part of its own population—are preventing the German Democratic Republic from getting on its feet. It would be misleading to depict its people as contented with their lot; they are not. But the economic improvement compared with three or four years ago is apparent at a glance in the street scene of a dozen towns, the look of the children on their way to school, the traffic on the roads, the crowds in the cafés and theaters.

Only the agricultural scene is superficially unchanged. In East as in West Germany, industry is the dominant interest, and the first beneficiary of a change for the better is the industrial population. The workers' and peasants' state seems to manage its peasants no better than the so-called capitalists' and landlords' state did. The grievances of the country people are still serious. The grievances that are aired in the towns—and they are still aired very readily—are of a relative kind; in effect, everything Western is considered to be superior to the products offered on the Socialist market.

For very many products, this belief is still well founded. Socialist television sets have small screens; Socialist gear-boxes wear out too quickly, for lack of hard steels; Socialist coffee is old and tired and very expensive; Socialist films are dreary and Socialist newspapers unreadable. These grumbles do not compare with the bitter complaints of five years ago. Bottlenecks have been overcome; industry is productive; there is plenty to eat and drink and plenty to buy with the high wages that the industrial worker can earn, or with the good salaries that are open to the technicians, managers and intellectuals so long as they are on good terms with the state. What used to be the special standard of consumption provided in Leipzig for the Fair is now expected generally and, but for the occasional slip, generally provided.

The source of this relative well-being is precisely the same in East as in West Germany. For all its misfortunes, East Germany was left with a pool of technical skill and of basic industrial equipment sufficient to secure it a place in the Communist economic world not dissimilar to that of West Germany in the Western world. With a substantial part of the mechanical engineering industry (as well as of the chemical, electrical, and optical industries) of the former German Reich, the German Democratic Republic is prospering as a supplier primarily of investment and production goods, primarily to the Communist bloc with its insistent demand for machinery, machine tools, and industrial installations. The basic resource, as it has turned out, was the human skill. It is not only in the West that the Germans have contrived, after a period of stagnation and gloom, to reequip their dismantled factories better than new and reestablish an urban standard of living. Labor is short; but productivity—though still well below that of West Germany—has risen as the new machines have come in. . . .

Unfortunately, no improvement in the temper of East German politics has accompanied the economic recovery. An effort in that direction was made last year by the group headed by Herr Schirdewan, Herr Oelssner, and Herr Wollweber. Herr Schirdewan appears, from the general answers that are given in Berlin to a tactless foreign questioner, to have pressed for a general policy less calculated to widen the breach between the East and West German states than is the present policy of Herr Ulbricht. Herr Oelssner is said to have desired an economic policy less ruthlessly set on squeezing out the small surviving private interests. Herr Wollweber found himself in the curious position of a chief of the security services seeking to abate the severity of the police system. It is in the logic of things that an eventual alternative East German government might have some such program as this, and there were indications that the Russians for a time last year were inclined to give Herr Schirdewan some support; but if they were, in January they withdrew it and the dissidents were expelled from their offices in the party and the state. Some of the economic reforms that they desired seem, nevertheless, to be going through; but in politics, and in particular in all-German questions, the Ulbricht line is more severely in force than ever.

The days are gone when East German Communists would impress on the foreigner their earnest desire for the reunification of their country. Germany, they now say is not going to be united at the expense of the German Democratic Republic; an attempt by Bonn to extend its system to East Germany would mean world war; the most that can be done is the so-called "confederative" solution, which, when explained, boils down to no more than an all-German advisory council, each of the two German governments retaining all its powers, including its separate foreign relations and its separate armed forces. This bland requirement of an indefinite shelving of the problem of German unity might be taken as the expression of a reviving self-confidence, which the present rate of East German economic progress could very well be held to justify—if it were not accompanied by a crescendo of hostile propaganda against the West generally and West Germany in particular. The tone of the East German press and radio, and indeed of party spokesmen individually (civil and helpful as they are to a seriously interested visitor) is truly terrifying. Bonn, in particular, is spoken of constantly as a hostile power resolved to seize power in the East by armed attack.

This atmosphere has been made worse than ever by the West German government's disclosure . . . of its intention to accept atomic weapons. It is the custom of the East German press, radio, and politicians to portray Dr. Adenauer and his ministers as the successors of Hitler, Goering and Goebbels. When the Bundestag foreign affairs debate from March 21 to 25 turned into a debate on atomic rearmament, the East German population was drenched daily and hourly with commentaries and denunciations on the bloodthirsty schemes of Bonn. People receive this, in general, skeptically enough, with an imperviousness induced by years of tedious exhortation. The regime has not learnt how to make itself believed, much less loved; still, it is making itself accepted as permanent.

EAST GERMAN ECONOMIC REVIVAL [9]

The West ought not to conclude that there is no East German recovery at all. . . . The recovery is assuming striking proportions.

[9] From "Dogma and Practice," article by a special correspondent. *The Economist.* 187:323-4. April 26, 1958. Reprinted by permission.

Somewhat to the surprise of its inhabitants, the economy of the German Democratic Republic has turned into a going concern before their eyes.

The first years of the Communist experiment in East Germany were marked by a luxuriant crop of ambitious new projects, conceived with more regard for what was thought desirable than for what was possible. The then fashionable search for self-sufficiency within each state—discarded now that the international division of labor has been adopted as a good Communist principle—helped to lead the planners astray. In the general pursuit of dogmatic ends, too many and too big things were attempted at once, and the economy's urgent need for quick practical repair of its working parts was neglected.

The last five years have seen a considerable pruning and rationalization of the early designs; the planners have become less dogmatic and more flexible in their methods. Budgetary control has been made more real, and money has been used as an instrument for the tailoring of ideas to resources. Facts have been allowed to speak for themselves. There is now a reasonably good system of published statistics. As the economy gets going, the apparatus of central planning and control is being streamlined and made more flexible. Herr Ulbricht introduced in February a functional devolution of powers in the economic branches of the government; this reform, involving the abolition of seven industrial ministries and a large reduction in central government staffs, is being carried through at high speed, and there seems no doubt that it is intended to give the men actually engaged in running industry more initiative than they have had before. (In general the men at the top in East German industry are, of course, party men; as the grip of the ministries is loosened, the grip of the party is, if anything, tightened.)

In this less perfectionist atmosphere, a series of projects that not so long ago looked more showy than practical have been brought to serious fruition. Some of the most striking of them were designed to remedy specific disproportions arising out of the partition of Germany in 1945. Thus, the area that is now the German Democratic Republic was traditionally a heavy user, and a negligible producer, of iron and steel; according to the figures commonly quoted, before the partition the territory had 49 per cent of the German machine construction industry but only 3 per cent of the metallurgical industry. In seeking to create a new iron and steel industry to fill part of the gap in supplies, the East German planners had the further difficulty that, while their state is the world's biggest producer of brown coal, its hard coal production and therefore its metallurgical coke production are very small. No high-grade iron ore is produced domestically.

The efforts made to remedy these disproportions are a sharp reminder that German industrial eminence is not confined to the Federal Republic. Brown coal production is being expanded on a huge scale; this is relatively simple, since the deposits are there and are accessible, but it does require very large excavators and elaborate handling installations, which are being produced and put into service. A process for producing metallurgical coke from brown coal has been developed at Lauchhammer, north of Dresden. Three briquetting plants process 6 million tons a year of brown coal under high pressure into 2 million tons of special-quality briquettes; these are delivered by conveyor belts to the Lauchhammer cokery, where they are further processed into 1 million tons of unusual-looking coke (700,000 tons of which is considered of metallurgical quality), together with coal gas and the usual by-products.

Brown coal coke from Lauchhammer is among the materials fed to another novel plant, at Calbe, near Dessau, designed by East German metallurgists to produce foundry iron on a large scale from very poor materials: Harz and Thuringian ores with brown coal ash (which contains iron), brown coal coke, and an admixture of gasworks coke. The ten blast furnaces, smaller and lower and designed for very different charging, combustion and discharging conditions than the conventional blast furnace, produce about one hundred tons a day each; they supply the entire East German requirement of foundry iron, with a surplus for export. (Iron for steelmaking is produced from imported conventional materials by the Stalinstadt iron works near Frankfurt on the Oder.) The original plan for Calbe, which envisaged twenty furnaces, was found to be more than was needed; work on the second group of ten furnaces was stopped, and the installations, though partly built, are being scrapped and their site leveled. Any embarrassment felt about that piece of over-investment seems to be completely outweighed by satisfaction at the good performance of the plant as it now stands, and at the interest it has aroused in West Germany and abroad.

Another unexpected industrial sight is the Warnow-Werft shipyard at Warnemünde (Rostock). The Soviet zone of Germany included no important seaport and no important ship-building center; its seaborne trade was formerly carried through Hamburg (now West Germany) and Stettin (now Poland), and the German shipbuilding centers on the Baltic were Stettin and Danzig. Rostock is to be the new center for shipping and shipbuilding; preparatory and dredging work has just begun on a new port, to take ships up to 10,000 tons, in the salt lake called the Breitling at the mouth of the Warnow. Across the Breitling from the pine wood which now marks the harbor site, a new shipyard has been built where there was formerly a private yard building small boats and repairing fishing craft. The new yard has an orderly layout and ample space for sectional assembly. Its labor force is mostly young, recruited from other occupations and trained on the spot. All the overhead crane operators are women. Most of the technical staff are under thirty and come from the shipbuilding faculty at Rostock; the director is thirty-six.

These three plants are all in one way or another showpieces; but a visit to some of the mechanical engineering centers of Saxony and Thuringia leaves no doubt that the traditional skills of what used to be central Germany are still there, and are hard at work in reequipped factories. At the former Wanderer works at Chemnitz (now called Karl-Marx-Stadt), from which the Russians removed virtually everything that the bombers had failed to destroy, highly automatic machine tools are being turned out in series with 98 per cent of new machines. The East Germans are well-equipped with the means for their own reequipment. Defeat, revolution and emigration have left them still an advanced industrial country which can be seen, through the clouds of dogma, once more fully at work.

SOVIET AIMS IN EAST GERMANY [10]

Bulking large in the new East-West crisis over Berlin is a relentless and untiring drive by Moscow to force the Western Allies to recognize the political existence of the East German Communist regime—a regime which is commonly described in Western quarters as a Soviet "puppet" government, a gang of Russian "hirelings," or a band of Soviet "marionettes."

Khrushchev's sensational announcement that he will relinquish Russia's rights in Berlin to the East German Reds [see next section—Ed.] constitutes the latest and most dramatic installment in a long series of moves by which the Soviets have been steadily converting the East German Communist regime into a sovereign establishment.

The ability of the United States, Great Britain and France to deter this process has been so limited that it has long become a practice for the West to fire off a salvo of contemptuous adjectives to accompany each progressive entrenchment of the East German Red regime—and basically to be obliged to let it go at that.

As a result, the West has come to draw a sharp distinction between the East German Communist government with which it refuses to deal and the similar Soviet-imposed Communist regimes in the rest of Eastern Europe whose political existence it has reluctantly recognized.

The facts are that the East German Red government is scarcely more and scarcely less of an impostor, usurper and band of Soviet marionettes and hirelings than are the Communist governments of, say, Hungary, Rumania and Bulgaria, to take the simplest cases.

All of these regimes, like the East German government, were installed by Soviet military power. None of them would last more than a few weeks if they were not directly or indirectly sustained by Soviet military might. Each of them is as thoroughly detested by their enslaved populations as is the East German Red regime.

[10] From "Crisis Welcome to East Germans," by Gaston Coblentz, correspondent. New York *Herald Tribune*. p 1. November 10, 1958. Reprinted by permission.

One of the cardinal differences between these three other satellite regimes and the East Germans is that the Soviets have erected the East German government in a part of a nation— that is, the eastern part of Germany covering some 40 per cent of German territory and ruling over about 30 per cent of the total German population—whereas Hungary, Rumania and Bulgaria are still, except for some post-war territorial readjustments, geographically intact.

German Reds' Status

However, the East German regime in fact rules over a considerably larger number of people—roughly 16 million—than, for example, Hungary or Bulgaria. It controls a larger industrial plant. Its Communist party has a more important history than the others, except for in some respects Bulgaria.

As regards subservience to Moscow, observers have for some time noted that the West has been inclined to exaggerate the servility of the East German Reds to the Kremlin. For at least three years there have been mounting indications that East German party chief Walter Ulbricht, one of the most unappetizing figures in the international Communist gallery, is not merely a passive recipient of Moscow's orders, but on occasions appears to exert considerable pressure on the Kremlin on important party and state issues.

Ulbricht a Power

His influence appears to have grown rather than decreased after the near-destruction of his regime in the violent East German anti-Communist uprising of 1953. In respect to party matters, Ulbricht was, for example, a striking standout among Communist leaders of Eastern Europe in his refusal to ape Khrushchev's short-lived anti-Stalinist campaign two years ago. At a moment when violent attacks on Stalin became the vogue throughout the Soviet bloc, Ulbricht definitely continued to hallow Stalin's memory.

In state questions his influence has been felt in the Soviet proposal for a confederation between the East German and West German governments. There are many signs that this particu-

lar formulation was originated by Ulbricht and his associates
and subsequently adopted by Khrushchev.

Against this background, the West's insistence on non-recognition of the East German regime was long closely linked to
the idea of dictating a settlement of the German question to
Russia from a position of Western strength.

The essence of that concept was that the Communists would
succumb to Western demands for free elections in all of Germany and agree to liquidation of the East German government.

The Western Big Three's important alliance with Chancellor
Adenauer's Western Germany was also from the outset closely
linked to this idea. One of its vital ingredients was Western
recognition of the Bonn government as the sole legitimate representative of the German people.

That is still the steadfast official policy of Washington,
London and Paris. It would clearly be extremely dangerous to
attempt to revise or modify it. Any move by the Western
Big Three to recognize the East German Communist regime
would deal a body blow to the Western alliance with Bonn and
thus imperil one of the keystones of the Western defense system
in Europe.

West on Spot

Thus, with respect to the Western Big Three's position in
Berlin, the present situation is therefore not an enviable one.
It appears likely that no amount of Western verbal denunciation
of East German Communists will prevent the Kremlin from
turning control of Western traffic in and out of the city over
to the Ulbricht government. The West will probably be able
to continue avoiding diplomatic recognition of the East German
Reds. But de facto recognition of the grim essence of the situation is becoming increasingly difficult to escape.

IV. A NEW EAST-WEST SHOWDOWN?

EDITOR'S INTRODUCTION

When at the end of November 1958 Russia's Premier, Nikita Khrushchev, proposed that West Berlin become a "free city" by the withdrawal of Western troops, it soon appeared that he had in mind far broader questions than the fate of that single, important city. If he meant to reopen the entire German question which has inflamed the cold war since its inception, he could not have picked a more dramatic site. The Western Allies have not so soon forgotten the "airlift" to Berlin ten years ago, made necessary by the East's blockade of the city.

For many other reasons, some arising out of the unfinished business of World War II, Berlin may be a key to the partial resolution or greater intensification of the East-West cold war. In the articles which follow, the specific problem of Berlin is reviewed first. But back of this are deeper East-West issues concerning Germany which have been debated here and abroad since the war's end. These are surveyed next from the diverse points of view of the United States, Britain, Russia, and the Germans.

The current Russian proposals about Berlin are given in the first article. The challenge they offer to the United States is set forth in the next selection.

Former President Truman, who more than any other single person galvanized the West into resistance to the Berlin blockade of 1948-1949, offers his vigorous opinion that similar resistance is required again.

The United States, and other Western powers, reacted immediately to the Soviet proposal on Berlin indicating that they would resist unilateral Soviet pressure to oust them from the city. Later developments indicated they were prepared to enter negotiations with the Soviet Union on this matter as well as on the broader German question. Early in 1959, the State Department issued an analysis of the Soviet Note on Berlin which had reviewed German affairs since the war and before. Brief extracts from this analysis are reprinted here.

What the East and West have heretofore staked out as plans for Germany are then discussed by Arthur J. Olsen, New York *Times* correspondent. A short review of the actual official negotiations that have taken place between the Western powers and Russia over Germany is next given by Harry Schwartz, another *Times* correspondent.

In 1958 the German question, after a few years in which the debate about it had subsided, was suddenly projected anew into the political arena of various Western states, Germany and Britain especially, and the United States. These new discussions took place before the latest Russian proposal on Berlin. In large part they grew out of the interest in the idea of "disengagement" in Europe under which various plans were suggested whereby East-West forces might be withdrawn from Central Europe.

Even before 1958 the Polish Foreign Minister, Adam Rapacki, had proposed through official diplomatic channels that all atomic weapons and their production should be banned from the two Germanies, Poland, and Czechoslovakia. This ban would also have applied to Soviet and Western military installations in the area. Little came from the ensuing discussion of this idea which the United States, along with other powers concerned, rejected. The Polish Foreign Minister, however, again broached his plan at the end of 1958 in a modified version, explained in a New York *Times* dispatch.

Meantime another suggestion about disengagement came from the former United States Ambassador to Russia, George F. Kennan. His ideas, which he first gave over the British Broadcasting System, follow. They were roundly and quickly rejected by former Secretary of State Dean Acheson, and variously debated by other Americans. The views of James P. Warburg and Dr. George N. Shuster are given here.

In Europe, the British Labour Party has been interested in similar ideas or policies and the party's leader, Hugh Gaitskell, comments on them next. A report of a debate in the British House of Commons indicates that the German question is a live political issue in Britain and that the Conservative government is preparing to make new proposals about Germany in the near future.

The article by Terence Prittie, the *Manchester Guardian* correspondent in Bonn, attempts to divine what the Russians may be aiming at in their Berlin proposals. The author believes that the Russians may in fact have abandoned the idea of German reunification.

The next to last article, from Bonn's Ambassador in Washington—stating the case against disengagement—can be considered the official West German position at this time.

Recent developments regarding Western Allied policy on Berlin are summarized in the concluding item, an editorial from the *Christian Science Monitor*.

A NEW RUSSIAN PROPOSAL ON BERLIN [1]

The Soviet Union proposed [on November 27, 1958] that West Berlin become a free city, independent of both East and West Germany, completely demilitarized and with its own government.

The Soviet Government promised that, if the West agreed to this, the Soviet would honor West Berlin's independence and secure for it "unhampered communications" with the East and the West.

In proposing this, Moscow expressly denounced the wartime agreements providing for Big Four occupation of Berlin and Germany.

It served notice that all Soviet occupation functions, including control over the West's access routes to West Berlin, would be turned over to the East German Government in six months.

In return for the Soviet guarantee of Berlin's communications, West Berlin would have to pledge not to permit "subversive activities" against the Communist bloc on its territory, Moscow said.

[1] From "Moscow Proposes West Berlin Be Free City," by Max Frankel, correspondent. New York *Times.* p 1+. November 28, 1958. Reprinted by permission.

If the Western powers reject the free city proposal, "there will no longer exist any subject for talks between the former occupying powers on the Berlin question," the Government declared.

Moscow seemed to leave no doubt that the decision to give East Germany "full" rights over its territory and air space by June 1 was final and not subject to negotiation.

Failure of the West to "recognize" this decision would be to reply in "the language of crude force," Moscow asserted.

It warned that any future "violations of the borders" of East Germany would be regarded here as aggression against the Communist camp and would immediately evoke appropriate retaliation. . . .

In . . . a news conference . . . on November 27 Premier Nikita S. Khrushchev emphasized the importance he attached to the Soviet action. . . .

He insisted that Moscow was not using the "form of an ultimatum." But, he said, the Soviet Union has "no other way out."

In arming West Germany and thus violating the Potsdam Agreement, the Western powers paid no attention to Soviet protests, the Premier declared.

Since the West's rights in Berlin derive from three-power and four-power agreements at the end of World War II, there now prevails "an obviously absurd situation" of the Soviet Union seeming to support Western activities against the Soviet Union and its Communist allies, Moscow said.

The Government declared that it "cannot tolerate such a situation any further."

It therefore is giving "notice" that it considers "null and void" the agreement of September 12, 1944, between the United States, Britain and the Soviet Union delineating the zones of occupation in Germany and providing for the joint administration of Berlin, as well as the agreement of May 1, 1945, among the United States, Britain, France and the Soviet Union, establishing control machinery for the occupation of Germany and Berlin.

Both agreements preceded the Potsdam conference of the Big Four heads of government in July 1945, which ratified the war-time occupation plans.

In its note to West Germany, Moscow also referred to the Western powers' contention that their right to access to West Berlin stems from the fact of Germany's capitulation and occupation. This is completely unfounded, especially since two independent Germanies have already been in existence for more than nine years, Moscow contended.

The Soviet note to the Western Big Three said the Moscow government planned "at an appropriate moment" to begin negotiations with East Germany to transfer to it all the functions hitherto performed by Soviet authorities under the now-renounced agreements.

It will defer this transfer for six months to give the Big Four time to arrange the free city proposal for West Berlin, Moscow went on. If a half-year goes by without agreement, however, then the Soviet Union will simply complete its arrangements with East Germany alone, it said.

Since West Berlin is completely surrounded by East German territory this move will make the Western powers' continued access to the city dependent on the tolerance of the East German government—a government they do not recognize and with which they have consistently refused to deal.

Moscow said that Western occupation of West Berlin was damaging to Soviet security interests. It would be highly unlikely therefore that East Germany would agree after next June to keep open the present military corridors from West Germany to West Berlin, even if the Western powers decided to deal with it.

The Soviet plan thus amounted to notice that Western troops would have to quit West Berlin in the next six months or have their supply lines sealed off.

Moscow maintained that all of Berlin was rightfully East German territory. It said it had offered the free city plan, however, as a "sacrifice," which it said proved the Communist bloc's desire not to annex any territory.

Since West Berlin is now committed to a capitalist system, Moscow is willing to recognize reality and to grant the inhabitants of West Berlin the right to any social system they wish, Moscow went on. Both Germany and the Big Four should pledge to refrain from all interference with a free city of Berlin, the Soviet note suggested.

The Soviet Union contended that West Berlin would have greater prosperity as a free city than at present. It promised to give it orders for industrial goods in amounts large enough to insure the city a stable economy and offered also to sell it "necessary" raw materials and food on a "commercial basis."

The Soviet Government did not specify the kind of subversive activities that it expected would be outlawed in the proposed free city. But Mr. Khrushchev said that while there would be nothing to discuss with the West if the free city plan were rejected, he was prepared to clarify all points if the West showed any interest.

If the free city plan is rejected by the West, it would not stop us, the Premier asserted. He said there was no point in questioning Moscow's resolve to end the occupation of Berlin and the Soviet note showed impatience with any suggestion that Soviet plans could be ignored.

If the suggestion of non-recognition "covers an intention to draw the world into a war over Berlin, the advocates of such a policy" should realize that they were assuming "an extremely grave responsibility" before the nations and before history, the note said.

The Communist nations of Europe will act on the motto "One for all, all for one," the Government declared. It said they would respond to any acts of aggression and included in that definition any violations of the borders of East Germany or any other member of the Communist alliance.

Moscow said the "best" solution of the Berlin problem would be to return to the Potsdam principles forbidding the armament of Germany. It said this would mean the withdrawal of West Germany from the Atlantic Alliance and of East Germany from the Warsaw Treaty and an agreement forbidding either half of the country from having troops beyond those needed to keep order.

But the premise of Moscow's note was that the West would not be likely to agree to such a plan. The Soviet government again declared its readiness to negotiate a peace treaty with Germany. It said it would never consent to the country's reunification if this meant the swallowing-up of the East German Communist regime.

The Soviet Government recalled the damage suffered by France and Britain in World War II in an appeal for support in those countries. Its note to West Germany also said that West Berlin was now an economic burden and a drain on the West German budget. This situation would end once West Berlin became a free city, Moscow contended.

THE CHALLENGE TO THE UNITED STATES [2]

Premier Nikita S. Khrushchev's proposals for the future of Berlin are part of a subtle and ingenious new pattern of Soviet policy in Europe. This policy is focused initially on Berlin. But the ultimate Russian objective is what it has always been— the unification and neutralization of Germany. The Berlin proposals can only be understood when they are considered as part of the policy pattern and as a step toward this Soviet goal.

Two important factors emerged from the Russian action and Western reaction. One is the enormous confidence of the Soviet Union in challenging the West in Europe. For Europe is an area of the North Atlantic Treaty Organization which, despite its difficulties, remains the most formidable of mechanisms designed by the West to check Soviet ambitions. Mr. Khrushchev is playing for very high stakes in an extremely sensitive area.

Since he is far from being a fool and dislikes failure, the West must assume that he is confident of success without the risk of war. Western diplomats must look for the basis of this confidence in the present condition of the Western Alliance and

[2] From "Khrushchev's Move Offers Challenge to U.S.," by Drew Middleton, correspondent. New York *Times.* p E3. November 30, 1958. Reprinted by permission.

the Russian assessment of the effect of these conditions on policy making.

The second factor is that despite the shock and alarm in the capitals of the West, some major move by the Soviet Union obviously has been developing for the past six weeks. As early as the middle of October British officials of experience and distinction in their field had concluded that the tremor that ran through Western Europe when fighting seemed near, over Quemoy and Matsu, would embolden Mr. Khrushchev to test the strength of the Atlantic Alliance by renewing pressure on Berlin.

This has been done. But it is only the starting point for a much longer and more widespread operation. This will embrace the presentation by the Soviets of the Rapacki plan for an atom-free zone in central Europe, continued manipulation of the Soviet positions at two disarmament conferences in Geneva to give the impression of a reasonable Russian compromise and an effort by Moscow to warn the smaller members of the Atlantic Alliance against the danger of providing the West German Army with tactical atomic arms.

Here and at every other point the Soviet policy trail leads back to Germany. Mr Khrushchev made it abundantly clear in his note . . . that he wants further development of relations between West and East Germany leading eventually to a confederation of the two nations. One way of achieving this is by raising the status of East Germany in the eyes of the West Germans and their allies. This he is attempting to do.

This is an old story. But it is no older, and it may strike some Europeans as a distinctly more practical means of uniting Germany, than Chancellor Adenauer's contention, in which he is supported by the West, that unity can result only from free elections all over the country. No one, except Dr. Adenauer, appears to believe there is the slightest chance that this will occur, given the character of Soviet policy. Since modern weapons rule out the use of force, the Germans, East and West, can look forward only to a division of their nation as long as this policy is followed.

Areas for Maneuver

Comparisons between the situation in June of 1948 when Stalin's Russia began the blockade of Berlin and the present are useless because of one vital difference. Total blockade was the only policy position then assumed by the Soviet Union. Today the Russians can bargain on other policies within their general pattern.

Does the West want agreement on controlled cessation of nuclear tests? The Soviet Union will hint at accommodation if it can have some assurances the West German Bundeswehr will not be armed with tactical nuclear weapons. Are Washington, Paris, London and Bonn worried about what would happen to the "free city" of Berlin isolated in a sea of Soviet arms? Well, the Russians can say, consider the Rapacki plan [see "A Polish Plan," in this section, below—Ed.] or even the proposals put forward for military disengagement in Central Europe by Hugh Gaitskell, leader of the British Labour Party. [See "A British Labourite View," in this section, below—Ed.]

These proposals, the Russians can say, would, if accepted, remove the danger to Berlin by removing the armies of the East and West from Germany.

The offer of the status of free city to Berlin is bait. Mr. Khrushchev knows that the West would not trust either the Russians or the East German Communists to honor the status of the free city for a second more than it suited them. But in his portfolio are other proposals that would remove troops from the area and "guarantee" Berlin's status. And if that happened, the Russians could argue, there is really no reason why the West and East Germans could not move steadily toward confederation.

There is one serious weakness in the present Western position on Germany. Out of deference and respect to Chancellor Adenauer's demands, members of the NATO alliance have made few contacts with the East Germans. These contacts have been left to the Germans and there are many more of them beyond the routine meetings of low rank civil servants dealing with railroads and canals and minor trade arrangements. There is a strong possibility that in embracing the idea of confederation between the two Germanies Mr. Khrushchev believes he is advocating a policy that has considerable support in West Germany outside the Chancellery in Bonn.

The series of firm negatives that resounded in Washington, London, Paris and Bonn in answer to Mr. Khrushchev's proposals are important but not the only part of the Western reaction to the new pattern of Soviet policy. For the Soviet Union's proposals on Berlin, on disengagement and on nuclear test suspension are directed to a wider audience. In preparing its approach on these policies the Soviet Union is thinking, too, of the smaller NATO states. Even before the Berlin proposals were published the Poles were hawking the Rapacki plan to Denmark and Norway.

Disunity in NATO

The dimensions of the new Soviet pattern emerged when the Western Alliance showed signs of disunity. For more than a year differences have been developing among NATO members over Cyprus, Icelandic fishing limits and German nuclear rearmament.

The immediate diplomatic problem of the leaders of the alliance is the presentation to Europe of an alternate plan to that proposed by Khrushchev. It will not be enough to tell the NATO countries that the West will only consider German reunification on Western terms and that the German army is to get tactical atomic weapons.

This would almost certainly lead to Russian denunciation of Washington and London for refusing an amicable settlement of the German problem and to warnings, done in Moscow's best flesh-creeping style, that the other Allies would have to share the consequences of American and British intransigence. There are plenty of signs that it would be a misjudgment to believe that the European members of the alliance will continue to accept a Western policy on Germany whose inflexibility periodically sets alarm bells ringing.

Support for Talks

No one is talking appeasement on Germany or anywhere else. But if Khrushchev continues to suggest negotiations with the Americans, the British and French on Berlin and East Germany, strong support for some sort of conference is likely to develop. Even the British, a civil servant remarked this week, probably would "go along" if there seemed to be some prospect of progress in talks with the Soviet Union.

Vice President Nixon, in one of his speeches during his . . . [November 1958 visit to Britain] remarked that the citizen of London who has been bombed is likely to have views different from those of the American who has not. This difference extends to all Western Europe. It is one reason why, in the coming months of diplomatic activity, Europe generally will be more responsive to proposals for a conference than the United States.

PRESIDENT TRUMAN'S ADVICE [3]

The United States, Great Britain and France should inform the Soviet Union that any attempt to compel the West to abandon Berlin by the use of the puppet government of East Germany will not work and will be resisted.

The use of a slave government, imposed by Russia on the people of East Germany, to dispose of our rights in Berlin is an act of mockery and cynicism and a move fraught with danger.

Whether this move to compel the United States, Great Britain and France to deal with the East Germans on Berlin is a maneuver to force recognition of East Germany or merely another try in a series of provocative acts to harass the West, we cannot permit them to get away with it.

There is a peaceful solution to the German problem as there is a peaceful solution to every international problem, if the Russians will abandon their relentless tactics of keeping the world in turmoil and probing how far they can bully us while

[3] From "If We Stand Up to the Russians, They Will Back Down," by former President Harry S. Truman. © 1958 by North American Newspaper Alliance, Inc. Reprinted by permission. (Text from U.S. News & World Report. 45:76-7. December 5, 1958.)

yet escaping war. The real danger is that one of these days the Russians may go too far.

I, for one, see no valid reason to fear a united Germany now. I think Germany has learned her lesson after two catastrophic experiences and should take her place in the constructive and peaceful ways of other nations in mutual cooperation and development.

The immense talents of the German people and German science should be of great help in the development and improvement of the lot of people all over the world. This is where Russia could be of much help to hasten the betterment of the lot of all mankind if only she would apply her energies and new industrial development to the ways of peace.

But, as matters stand, we all have reason to fear a Russia now resuming the tough line of Stalinism, and more menacingly so because of her recent successes in the field of military science. East Germany under Russian domination is not a buffer state for peace but is, in fact, a steppingstone for Russian invasion westward. A Germany united could be a bulwark for peace in Europe. What Russia really is after, I believe, is a division of Germany, with East Germany a permanent part of the Russian cluster of satellite states.

The Russian move to pull out of East Berlin—ostensibly to emphasize East Germany's ability to govern itself—is an act of diplomatic buffoonery because Russia continues to occupy East Germany with an enormous army of over 450,000 soldiers and will not allow the people of East Germany to elect a government of their own choosing.

Communist Russia continues to violate the agreements at Potsdam by which Poland, Hungary, Rumania and Bulgaria were to be allowed to choose their own forms of government in free elections. It is now thirteen years since the Russians made this agreement with us in Potsdam, and the people of these countries remain under Russian total domination and guns.

I read that Khrushchev has repeated some old suggestions to recent travelers to Russia that the two German states—West Germany and East Germany—should be left to negotiate their union without the participation of the United States, Great

Britain, France and Russia. This is a design to expose West Germany to Communist conquest.

We cannot abandon West Berlin to the Communists, no matter what the risks. For, if we do, we might as well abandon all of free Europe. There is no minimizing the situation created by the return of the Kremlin to the hard, ruthless and bullying methods of Stalin. In this situation the United States, Great Britain and France must stand together in closest harmony.

I know from past experience that, if we stand up resolutely to the Russians when they are bent on mischief, they will back down. We must meet each situation the Communists provoke, even if we have to use force to meet force. We once kept the lines open to Berlin by air, in face of tremendous hardships. Of course, we could do it again, even if the odds are greater now. There are other ways and avenues of supplying West Berlin, including certain routes over land and water, which I considered when I ordered the airlift into Berlin [in 1948].

At that time I called on the military chiefs for reccmmendations on how we could supply West Berlin.

We were going to supply West Berlin, whatever the risks.

We could not yield to Russia without exposing all of Europe to further Russian encroachments. There were sharp differences of opinion among the military as to the degrees of risk involved in the various methods of running the blockade.

There were those in the Air Force who were hesitant because of the narrowness of the air corridor, the limited air strips and the prodigious amounts of tonnage that had to be flown. Fear was also expressed of possible interference from hostile planes; and the weather was bad.

I turned to the Army. The Army said it was prepared to send armed convoys and armored trains at once into Berlin through the blockade. I turned to the staff of the air command and said: "If you don't think you can handle this task, I will turn the job over to the Army."

Whereupon the air chiefs came to a quick resolution and said that they would take full responsibility for supplying West Berlin by air, starting that day, and calling up all available craft and personnel. The rest is history.

What Stalin Promised at Potsdam

When Churchill and Attlee, Stalin and I met in Potsdam, we sought and got signed agreements on three major things:

First, we wanted, through a friendly joint occupation by the United States, Great Britain, France and Russia, to help shape a new Germany, one that would not again be a threat to the peace of Europe. We hoped to end the occupation without punitive retribution as soon as it was possible for a new and united Germany to take its place among nations, through a peace treaty.

Secondly, the United States, Great Britain, France and Russia agreed that free elections, through secret ballots, should take place in Poland, Rumania, Hungary and Bulgaria so that these countries might have governments of their own choosing.

Our third, and perhaps our most pressing concern at that time, was to get Russia to come into the war against Japan and thus hasten the end of the war in the Pacific, which the top military leaders estimated might yet cost millions of lives.

Our anxiety about victory and the ending of the most destructive war in history impelled us to place some credibility on the word of Russia as an ally, despite growing evidence that Russia seemed determined to play a lone and expansionist hand. I had already warned Molotov [Soviet Foreign Minister] about Russia keeping her agreements.

But Russia occupied an open and important flank, and our concern was to get the war over with.

Russia took her time about opening up the front against the Japanese, as she had promised, waiting until the last moment, when victory was certain, to make only a token gesture. She expected that this last-minute appearance would enable her to join in the occupation of Japan.

But by this time we had already learned enough about Russia in the occupation of Berlin and Germany to know that Russia would not cooperate. I therefore made certain that only our forces would occupy Tokyo and Japan and that Russia was to be excluded from any active participation in the administration of Japan.

I am convinced that, if we had allowed Russia to take part in the occupation of Japan, the results would have been a divided Japan, used as a base for Communist intrigue, just as East Berlin and East Germany are being used.

We now have a new crisis in Berlin, and our government must not give any sign of hesitation. I am glad that the Administration is taking a firm stand. I would reject any "summit" meeting with the Russians at this time, but I would call a meeting of our allies, to be fully prepared not only to meet but to anticipate the next Kremlin moves.

THE UNITED STATES REACTION [4]

On November 27, 1958, the Government of the Union of Soviet Socialist Republics handed the United States Ambassador in Moscow a communication relating to Berlin.

Similar notes were given by the Soviet government to the ambassadors of France, the United Kingdom and the Federal Republic of Germany.

In essence the Soviet notes demanded that the United States, the United Kingdom and France abandon West Berlin.

In its note the Soviet government has rewritten history and presented an account of the past which persons who have lived through the periods discussed will find difficult to recognize. Alterations have been effected in two ways—by omission and by distortion.

The succeeding pages aim to supply the more important Soviet omissions and correct the more obvious distortions contained in the Soviet note. . . .

Prewar Developments

Soviet Allegations

The Soviet note states that prior to World War II the Soviet Union displayed constant willingness to establish cooperation with

---

[4] From *Soviet Note on Berlin: An Analysis*, booklet issued by the United States Department of State. (Department of State Publication 6757) The Department. Washington 25, D.C. p 1-53. January 1959. (Excerpts as reprinted in the New York *Times*. p4. January 8, 1959.)

the other powers with the object of resisting Hitlerite aggression and that, if the Western powers had not been shortsighted in their hopes of turning Hitler eastward and had cooperated with the Union of Soviet Socialist Republics millions of lives would have been saved.

The Facts Are

1. The U.S.S.R. established diplomatic relations with Germany in 1923 and assisted in building up a new German war machine which had been prohibited by the Versailles Treaty after World War I.

2. From 1930 to 1933 the Soviet Union, through its international Communist arm, the Comintern, directed the German Communist party to collaborate with the Nazis and other extremists in undermining the German Weimar Republic. It helped sabotage democratic parties and institutions and promoted lawlessness and disorder. This aided Hitler's rise to absolute power.

3. In 1933, after Hitler came to power, the U.S.S.R. and Germany exchanged ratifications of an extended neutrality pact.

4. The U.S.S.R. signed six credit and commercial agreements with Germany between 1922 and 1933. During Hitler's ascendancy after 1933 the U.S.S.R. concluded twelve more agreements with the Nazi regime at the time when Hitler was building up his military power.

5. The U.S.S.R. turned aside from negotiations with the United Kingdom and France in August, 1939, and concluded the Molotov-Ribbentrop agreements which provided the necessary guarantees for coordinated Nazi-Soviet aggression in Eastern Europe and resulted in World War II.

6. In spite of warnings from the Western powers of impending German attack, the Soviet Government aided Nazi Germany until Hitler marched against it in 1941.

7. In April 1941, the U.S.S.R. signed a neutrality pact with the Japanese ally of Hitler, thereby clearing the way for the Pearl Harbor attack on the United States on December 7, 1941.

8. The United States, the United Kingdom and Canada provided large quantities of vital war materials to the U.S.S.R. during the war. This aid underscored prompt political support from the United States the day after Hitler attacked Russia in June 1941.

World War II and Postwar Developments

Soviet Allegations

The Soviet note states that the Western Allies had a "joint concerted policy" toward Germany in World War II. It maintains that, if these policies had been continued, as inaugurated by President Roosevelt, there would have been peaceful coexistence after the war. Instead, according to the Soviet note, the atmosphere was poisoned by Winston Churchill and others seeking an aggressive course against the U.S.S.R.

The Facts Are

1. In wartime agreements the Allied nations stated two fundamental policies: they pledged to defeat the enemy, and they declared they would strive for recovery from the war, continuing wartime cooperation.

2. A heavy price was paid to defeat the enemy.

3. Instead of implementing the wartime agreements, the U.S.S.R. proceeded to carry out its own plans for Communist expansion in Eastern Europe and prevented or delayed wherever possible the actions of the Western powers to promote economic recovery in Germany and all of Europe.

4. These Soviet actions, which contradicted Soviet pledges, destroyed the good will felt for the U.S.S.R. and convinced Western governments of the need for defense against Soviet expansionism.

5. Stalin declared the "cold war" on the West in 1946 by asserting that the wartime alliance with the West was dictated by expediency. He predicted wars between capitalist states and said the Communists would achieve domination over other people.

Postwar Relations With Germany

Soviet Allegations

The Soviet note charges the Western Allies with violation of the political and economic provisions of the inter-Allied agreements, particularly the Potsdam Agreement. It contends that these violations were a part of the Western "aggravation of the ideological struggle" and Western "war preparations." The Western Allies, it says, worked actively to prevent the peaceful unification of Germany and West Germany's leaders were militarists who made plans to unify Germany by force.

The note goes on to state that East Germany is governed under a constitution in "the finest progressive traditions of the German nation" and has made great "democratic and social gains." The Western powers, it states, used their presence in West Berlin to "pursue subversive activity" against Russia and the satellites, whereas, by contrast, the quadripartite agreement on Berlin was "scrupulously observed by the Soviet Union."

The note claims that, during the entire postwar period, despite aggravations and war preparations by the West, the Soviet Union remained a firm supporter of policies of "peaceful coexistence," "non-interference" in the affairs of other states, and respect for the "sovereignty and territorial integrity" of other countries. . . .

The Facts Are

1. The stated purposes of postwar agreements between the Allies on Germany were to eliminate vestiges of the Third Reich, to prevent rebirth of aggressive forces, and to chart a course by which Germany could recover its respect and play a constructive role in international affairs.

2. Long before the signature of the Potsdam Protocol, embodying these principles, in August 1945, the U.S.S.R. began its efforts to turn Germany into a Soviet satellite. It selected, trained and repatriated individuals who later became the political and military leaders of the East German regime.

3. Before the Western powers occupied their sectors in Berlin, the Soviet Army had licensed political parties and sub-

jected them to control through traditional Communist mechanisms. These still obtain in East Germany today.

4. Nevertheless the victorious powers negotiated the Potsdam Protocol, which contained both negative features (demilitarization, denazification, and reparations) and positive features (elected local governments, unified administration, democratic rights for all citizens, balanced economic treatment and an eventual peace treaty to settle the war). The U.S.S.R. refused to carry out these positive principles.

5. The United States did not wish Germany to become a Soviet satellite. It urged economic recovery in Europe as a whole.

6. The U.S.S.R. sidestepped an American proposal for a forty-year nonagression pact guaranteeing against a recurrence of German military aggression. The Soviets opposed economic recovery in Europe. They walked out of the four-power Allied Control Council for Germany and instituted the Berlin blockade in 1948 to try to force the Western Allies out of the city.

7. In Berlin the Soviets forced the split in the city and set up a rump government in East Berlin to oppose the duly elected government of the city.

8. Despite the lack of Soviet cooperation, the Western powers proceeded to carry out the Potsdam Protocol in their own zones in West Germany. Following free elections and the adoption of an approved basic law (constitution), the Federal Republic was established.

9. The Soviets proclaimed the so-called German Democratic Republic in 1949. No free elections have ever been held.

10. The Communists continue to prevent free circulation of information and to control movement of citizens in East Germany and between East and West Germany. They justify this action on grounds of preventing "Fascist aggression" and "outside provocation" by "espionage agencies" in West Berlin.

Reparations

Soviet Allegations

The Soviet note says the Western powers began to follow a policy in Germany counter to the provisions of the Potsdam

Protocol about a year after the war. The note specifies this was due to a heated ideological struggle which reversed wartime cooperation. It charges that the Western powers refused to give the U.S.S.R. reparations due from Germany.

The Facts Are

1. The Potsdam Protocol provided that the U.S.S.R. should receive from the Western occupation zones 15 per cent of specified types of such industrial capital equipment as was unnecessary for the German peace economy *in exchange for an equivalent* value of food and other raw materials plus an additional 10 per cent without exchange. Payment of reparations should leave enough resources to enable the German people to subsist *without external assistance.* It also provided that Germany should be treated "as a single economic unit."

2. The Soviet Union did *not* deliver food and other raw materials in return for large shipments of capital equipment from the Western zones.

3. The United States suspended reparations shipments because of the failure of the Soviet Union to implement the Potsdam Protocol as a whole.

4. The Soviet Union continued to extract reparations from its zone at a time when the Western powers were forced to maintain a minimum economic level by financing imports to Germany. In effect, shipments of reparations to the U.S.S.R. at a time when the United States was supporting its own zone to make up deficiencies caused by Soviet violations of the Potsdam Agreement amounted to the U.S.S.R.'s collecting reparations from the United States.

Rearmament

Soviet Allegations

The Soviet note says that the Western powers are rearming West Germany, encouraging and restoring the forces which had built up Nazi military power. The Soviets maintain that this is a violation of the Potsdam Protocol and that the Soviet Union has been compelled to establish the Warsaw Pact as a defensive system.

The Facts Are

1. The United States in 1943, 1946 and 1947 proposed the negotiation first of a twenty-five-year and later of a forty-year treaty which would guarantee against resurgence of German militarism. The Soviet Union effectively killed the negotiations by dragging in numerous extraneous and controversial issues.

2. In the United States zone of Germany the United States carried out fully the demilitarization provisions of the Potsdam Protocol by 1950.

3. Beginning in 1948 the Soviets built up a sizable "police force" in its zone, arming it with military-type weapons and having it trained by former German army officers.

4. In 1954 (a year before an army was established in West Germany) 140,000 German military personnel were under arms in the Soviet zone plus a police force of 100,000. At this time West German police numbered 150,000, although there are three times as many people in West Germany as in East Germany.

5. The military forces of the Federal Republic are integrated into the North Atlantic Treaty Organization, which has purely defensive purposes within the framework of the United Nations. The Federal Republic has renounced aggressive purposes and accepted specific limitations on armaments. The Western powers have repeatedly assured the Soviet Union on these points.

THE OPPOSING VIEWS—EAST AND WEST [5]

Near the end of World War II the victorious Allied powers rejected the tempting idea of paring the mighty German nation into a patchwork of small, powerless states.

Almost at the same moment their experts, laboring in the interest of an efficient temporary occupation, were drawing lines across the map of Germany.

The postwar history of Germany is largely the record of attempts to erase those lines drawn in 1944 and 1945. Both the Soviet Union and the Western powers are openly dissatisfied with the record.

[5] From "Germany: The Opposing Views," by Arthur J. Olsen, correspondent. New York *Times.* p E5. November 30, 1958. Reprinted by permission.

Their individual efforts to change the map by propaganda and pressure have failed. They have made no progress in joint efforts—at the summit, in foreign ministers' meetings and at the expert level—to fulfill the wartime resolve to transform Germany into a peaceful, democratic and unmenacing nation. Their mutually exclusive formulas for the unification of Germany show that the two sides do not even agree on what those adjectives mean.

Soviet Unification Plan

The Soviet Union frankly holds that the only safe Germany is one responsive to the needs and guidance of Moscow. Moscow would be content to have a "neutralized" free West Germany, at least for the time being. But not even as bait for the West Germans is the Soviet Union ready to relax its grip on the part of Germany it already possesses.

Thus the Soviet "unification" proposes:

(1) Western recognition of the German Democratic Republic (East Germany) as a sovereign state.

(2) Western acceptance of the Soviet thesis that the four occupation powers are no longer responsible for the unification of Germany.

(3) Direct negotiations between the West German and the East German governments on the terms of unification.

(4) These negotiations to be based on certain pre-conditions, among them "confederation" without dissolution of the rival governments, preservation of Communist institutions in the Soviet zone, Bonn's withdrawal from the North Atlantic Alliance and the withdrawal of Western defense forces from the territory of the West German Federal Republic.

Western Unification Plan

Proposals put forth by the three Western Allies and the Bonn Government are based upon sound moral principles—from the Western point of view—and the seemingly clear language of the

Potsdam Declaration. They would also further the strategic and security interests of countries threatened by Soviet expansionism.

The West insists upon:

(1) Free voting throughout the zones and in Berlin to elect a Constituent Assembly.

(2) This Assembly would establish a central German government.

(3) This all-German government would negotiate a peace treaty with the victor powers in which the final disposition of the German territories now under Polish and Soviet administration would be made.

(4) The central German government would establish its own international relationships subject to such controls or commitments as might be written into the peace treaty.

Western Response to Russia

The United States, Britain, France and West Germany are united in a flat rejection of the Communist unification program.

On juridical grounds, they view it as a violation of the Potsdam Agreement, particularly its promise to grant all the German people political freedom and such basic rights as freedom of the press, assembly and religion.

On moral grounds, they consider it impossible to recognize the permanent suppression of some 18 million Germans under Communist dictatorship.

On strategic-security grounds they see as a consequence of unification on the Soviet terms the rollback of Western power behind the Rhine. Their military authorities say the withdrawal of United States military forces from the European Continent would almost certainly follow.

The forsaken Bonn Republic would have little choice but to make an accommodation with Moscow. Whether West Germany were communized in short order or only gradually over the years would make little difference. Its substantial industrial power would be exercised in harmony with Moscow. Chancellor Adenauer asserts that the Soviet bloc bolstered by West Germany's resources would be stronger than the combined free world.

Western Europe would be gravely weakened and its people would be impelled to consider coming to terms with the Soviet colossus looming over them.

A similar psychological collapse could be expected in the sovietized countries of Eastern Europe and in uncommitted nations elsewhere.

Soviet Response to the West

The prospect of a Germany reunified in freedom presents almost as grim a prospect to one who looks upon the world with the eyes of Premier Khrushchev.

A Germany reunified according to the Western formula would mean a two-hundred-mile rollback of the Soviet frontier in Europe. The twenty-two Russian divisions in East Germany would have to pull back to Poland or beyond. Advanced missile bases would be lost.

The Soviet Union's uneasy grasp on its satellite countries would be weakened. The facilities of East Germany, the most industrialized satellite, would be lost to the Communist bloc. The psychological effect upon the uncommitted peoples who are told by the Communists that Moscow rides the tide of history would be terrific.

Perhaps most important of all, the security of the Soviet Union would be seriously undermined. Moscow would expect the vengeful Germans to enter into a scheme with the United States and the other Western Allies to prepare a new war on the Soviet Union. West German "militarists" are already doing all they can to serve that end, Moscow holds. How long before a resurgent, united Germany, coveting lost territories in the East, would start a new *Drang Nach Osten?*

Dim Outlook

What chance has either side of getting its way with Germany in the foreseeable future? Those who appraise the situation agree that the answer must be: Very little indeed.

The balance of power between East and West is so even and the penalties of nuclear war so great that an attempted solution by force seems improbable.

Mr. Khrushchev seems to be convinced that time is on his side. His government is warring persistently and adroitly upon the nerves of the West Germans, notably in the present campaign against West Berlin. Indications are that the basic Soviet policy on Germany is to hold what it has and bide its time. Goaded by Soviet harassment, impatient to restore Germany's oneness, the West Germans, in Moscow's view, will some day abandon the West and accept the Soviet terms.

Chancellor Adenauer and most statesmen he meets in Allied council rooms advocate a similar policy to achieve the opposite goal.

Stand firm and resolute, they say. Offer the Soviet Union every reasonable guarantee of security. Be prepared for peace treaty negotiations seeking drastically to limit Germany's future freedom of action in the military field. Eventually Moscow will recognize that its unnatural tyranny in Europe has ceased to serve the national interest.

The Bonn-Washington "policy of strength" is not universally approved in West Germany. Within this Federal Republic, political parties representing 40 per cent of the people, according to election figures, call it a policy of despair.

Approach the Soviet Union with an open mind, anti-Adenauer forces say. Perhaps there is an acceptable middle ground between the Western and the Russian unification plans. It is madness to argue that time is on the Western side. With every passing day the partition of Germany becomes firmer and more difficult to overcome.

Can unification be achieved short of a collapse by either side or a decision of arms?

Experienced and hardheaded observers, venturing to look ahead a year or two, say: Not very likely. If the Soviet Union would consider exchanging the solid security guarantee of its twenty-two divisions manning the East German bastion for less tangible guarantees in a peace treaty, its spokesmen have given hardly a hint of it. On the contrary, Soviet policy in Germany seems to be growing more rigid.

The West Germans for their part have shown no sign of weakening seriously under pressure. The Adenauer government, goaded by the opposition, has been moving cautiously to dicker with the Soviet Union in search of a potential compromise. But accepting the Soviet conditions as a basis of negotiation is out of the question now, for the restive West German Socialists as well as for Dr. Adenauer.

If the feeling-out process now under way produces no compromise that would permit Germany to reunite as a free nation, will the German question have come to a dead end? Not necessarily.

The Soviet Union and the leading Western powers are engaged now at Geneva and in the United Nations in limited and hesitant negotiations of which the ultimate goal is a system of general international disarmament.

If it is achieved, Germany would assume a new aspect in the calculations of military men and strategists. Events outside of Germany would accomplish what the diplomats and psychological warriors have failed to do. There would be a new, and more promising, look at the German question.

EAST-WEST AGREEMENTS [6]

The Soviet Union's proposal . . . drastically to alter the current status of Berlin and its threat of unilateral action to that end in six months caused diplomats to restudy the legal bases of the Berlin situation now existing.

That restudy showed that the present Berlin situation had its roots in agreements reached between the Soviet Union and the Western Allies in two different periods.

The first, during and immediately after World War II, was an era in which the West thought primarily of Germany as an enemy whose military rebirth had to be prevented for all time.

[6] From "Basic Documents Behind the Struggle for Germany and Berlin," by Harry Schwartz, correspondent. New York *Times*. p E5. November 30, 1958. Reprinted by permission.

At the same time the West looked on the Soviet Union as a stanch ally whose cooperation and friendship were assumed for an indefinite future period.

The second, quite different period was in mid-1949, when agreements were reached under which the Soviet Union consented to lift its unsuccessful blockade of West Berlin, a blockade that had been frustrated by the Berlin airlift of 1948-49.

Rights of Conquest

Fundamentally the United States position in Berlin derives from the rights it gained in the conquest of Nazi Germany. Along with the other victorious powers it agreed to the military occupation of Germany, including the joint occupation of Berlin. Since the Hitler regime had been destroyed, there was no German government. Thus the victors instituted a military regime, one it was presumed would continue until a peace treaty was concluded with a new German government satisfactory to the victor nations. The continued joint occupation of Berlin is the last remnant within Germany of these arrangements, persisting because there has been no German peace treaty and no formation of a single government for all Germany satisfactory to all the former Allies who won World War II.

There follows a chronological summary of the negotiations and agreements about Berlin and related questions that have created the situation the Russians now threaten to destroy:

The October 1943 *Conference of Foreign Ministers in Moscow*: At this meeting the foreign ministers of the United States, Britain and the Soviet Union agreed in principle to joint responsibility for Germany and joint occupation of Germany. They set up the European Advisory Commission to help draw up common policy regarding postwar Germany and other problems.

Occupation Zones

The European Advisory Commission: This body, consisting of the late John G. Winant for the United States, Sir William Strang for Britain, and Fedor T. Gusev for the Soviet Union, worked from January 1944 to August 1945. By July 1944, there was clear agreement on two points: joint occupation of Berlin and the establishment of a Soviet occupation zone embracing East Germany up to the present Western boundary of Communist East Germany.

The basic agreement reached in the EAC, which last week was denounced by the Soviet Union, was that of September 12, 1944. This defined occupation zones for the United States, Britain and the Soviet Union in Germany as a whole and in Greater Berlin as a separate unit, providing also for joint administration of Berlin.

In addition, on November 14, 1944, the EAC reached agreement on the formation by the United States, Britain and the Soviet Union of an Allied Control Council to be the supreme authority for Germany as a whole, and for each military commander in chief to be the supreme authority, under orders of his government, in each nation's occupation zone.

No agreement guaranteeing Western access to Berlin was ever reached in the Advisory Commission.

The Yalta Conference of February, 1945: At this meeting, the heads of government of the United States, Britain and the Soviet Union ratified the two EAC agreements mentioned above. They also agreed that France should receive an occupation zone in Germany and that the French should participate in the Allied Control Council. The French role was more fully defined in a four-power agreement of May 1, 1945.

Germany's surrender, May 1945: By V-E Day, British and United States troops occupied Germany to the Elbe River and were much further east than had been envisaged in the occupation zone agreement developed by the Advisory Commission. On the other hand, the Russians were in sole control of Berlin. It was clear that the Soviet Union would not give the West a share of Berlin unless the West withdrew its forces from the substantial and rich German area Western troops had conquered but which had been promised to Moscow.

The Berlin Agreement of June 5, 1945: This agreement, signed by the British, United States, French and Soviet military commanders in Germany, announced that the four governments "hereby assume supreme authority with respect to Germany." The commanders issued a statement announcing the pattern of military rule and occupation of Germany and Berlin as agreed by the EAC in September and November 1944, including the French role as approved at Yalta.

The Potsdam Agreement of August 1945: This reiterated the June 5 agreement about zones and the control council, but made no mention of Berlin. It set up a list of occupation objectives, provided for German reparations, promised support for the Soviet seizure of northern East Prussia (now the Kaliningrad area of the Soviet Union) from Germany, and "pending the final determination of Poland's western frontier" put "under the administration of the Polish state" the area of Germany east of the Oder and Neisse Rivers.

Air Routes

The Air Corridor Agreement: On November 30, 1945, the Allied Control Council in Berlin agreed that three corridors for air travel between Berlin and West Germany should be set up and that flights along these corridors could proceed without advance notice.

The Jessup-Malik Agreement of May 1949: The Soviet blockade of Berlin began in June 1948, but its success was prevented by the Berlin airlift. In early 1949 the Soviet Government decided to lift the blockade and arrangements to do so were made in secret negotiations at the United Nations in New York between Dr. Philip C. Jessup of the United States and Yakov A. Malik of the Soviet Union. In return for lifting of the Soviet blockade on Berlin, the West agreed to end the retaliatory counter-blockade it had imposed on East Germany. Both sides agreed to convene a meeting of the Big Four Council of Foreign Ministers in Paris May 23, 1949.

The Foreign Ministers Agreement of June 1949: The Council of Foreign Ministers ratified the Jessup-Malik agreement. It also declared that to facilitate transport and communications among the different occupation zones and also between the zones and Berlin, "the occupation authorities, each in his own zone, will have an obligation to take the measures necessary to insure the normal functioning and utilization of rail, water, and road transport. . . ."

Sovereign Germany

The Convention of October 23, 1954: This document, concluded between the United States, Britain and France on one hand and the German Federal Republic, reserved all the first three powers' "rights and responsibilities . . . relating to Berlin" so that they would continue after establishment of the German Federal Republic as a sovereign state.

Soviet-East German Agreement of September 20, 1955: This agreement, which marked Soviet recognition of the "sovereignty" of the German Democratic Republic, reserved to the Soviet Army control of the movement of British, French and American military personnel and freight between West Berlin and West Germany.

There, legally, the matter of divided Berlin has rested. . . .

Within what is now recognized as Germany, only the divided status of Berlin remains as envisaged in 1945, but there remains also without clear legal sanction the Polish administration of former German territory and the Soviet rule over the former northern part of East Prussia.

A POLISH PLAN [7]

Poland made public today a new version of her plan for a central European zone free of atomic weapons and installations.

The new version divides the process of eliminating atomic weapons in central Europe into two stages and combines it with a proposal for a reduction of conventional armed forces.

Adam Rapacki, Polish Foreign Minister, said that the new plan was aimed at meeting Western objections that the original Polish proposal would leave the North Atlantic Treaty Organization without its "nuclear shield," but would maintain the superiority of Communist land forces in the area.

[7] From "Rapacki Proposes 2-Stage Plan for Atom Ban in Central Europe." New York *Times*. p5. November 5, 1958. Reprinted by permission.

M. Rapacki said that the new version had been approved by Poland's Communist allies as the maximum step toward meeting Western objections to the idea of an "atom-free" central European zone.

Original Plan Recalled

Under the original Polish plan all atomic weapons and their production would have been banned in Poland, Czechoslovakia and East and West Germany. This would have included the installations of the Soviet Union and the West in the area, as well as the armed forces of the central European governments themselves.

The West turned down the plan on the ground that it was a dangerous threat to its military security in the area.

At a news conference, M. Rapacki explained his idea of breaking the plan into stages.

In the first stage there would be a ban on the production of nuclear weapons in Poland, Czechoslovakia and East and West Germany, he said. An obligation would be undertaken not to build installations or give nuclear weapons to armies that did not have them.

Under the second stage, nuclear installations of the Soviet Union and the West in the area would come under the ban. But this second stage would not go into operation until there had been agreement on conventional disarmament in the zone.

"Appropriate measures of control" would accompany the whole process, according to M. Rapacki's outline.

The Foreign Minister said Poland would do some diplomatic contact work to try to gain support for the plan.

MR. KENNAN'S VIEWS [8]

An American has stirred up a storm of excitement in Europe over a new approach toward ending the "cold war."

[8] From "The Kennan Ideas That Are Stirring up Europe," excerpts from broadcasts by George F. Kennan, former United States Ambassador to Moscow. *U.S. News & World Report.* 44:69-71. January 10, 1958. Reprinted from *U.S. News & World Report,* an independent weekly news magazine published at Washington. Copyright 1958 United States News Publishing Corporation.

George F. Kennan, former United States Ambassador to the Soviet Union, is widely recognized as the author of the policy of "containing" the Soviet Union. This is the policy that lies at the base of present Western strategy.

Now Mr. Kennan is offering policies which are radically different from present United States and Western policy. Through a series of lectures and a round-table talk, Mr. Kennan touched off excited debates in Britain. The West Germans, too, are debating his suggestions, which last week shaped up as a major issue in their country.

Here, in Mr. Kennan's own words from his lectures, and the symposium, as broadcast by the British Broadcasting Corporation, you get answers to the questions that are being raised about his proposals. [The lectures referred to were the Reith lectures mentioned by later authors in this book—Ed.]

Just what is the Kennan plan?

Mr. Kennan: I didn't mean to propose a plan. . . . I was trying to tell governments what they ought to think about, not what they ought to do. . . .

How can we get at the basis of the issues underlying the cold war?

Mr. Kennan: I can conceive of no escape from this dilemma that would not involve the early departure of Soviet troops from the satellite countries. Recent events have made it perfectly clear that it is the presence of these troops, coupled with the general military and political situation in Europe, which lies at the heart of the difficulty.

Well, why don't the Soviet troops get out of Eastern Europe?

Mr. Kennan: This at once involves the German problem . . . so long as American and other Western forces remain in Western Germany. . . .

Can we consider the idea of withdrawing all American forces from the continent of Europe?

Mr. Kennan: Yes.

And withdrawing U.S. troops from Britain, too?

Mr. Kennan: I must say that personally I can't see why they couldn't be, with the course of time—perhaps not overnight. . . . I can conceive of many variations of a disengagement. You could withdraw to garrison areas in Germany, as a first step, or you could clear a zone in Germany. You could remove the troops from Germany, which has been proposed from the Russian side. Or you could remove them from Germany and Eastern European countries and a certain number of Western countries. . . . I would personally think that no disengagement would be worth while from our standpoint which did not involve the evacuation of Poland and Hungary.

Well, how would that leave Germany? United and with the West?

Mr. Kennan: Specifically, the Western governments have insisted that such an all-German Government must be entirely free to continue to adhere to the NATO Pact, as the German Federal Republic does today; and it is taken everywhere as a foregone conclusion that an all-German government would do just that.

Why shouldn't the Germans be permitted to join the West if they want to?

Mr. Kennan: Now the question at once arises as to what would happen. . . . The Soviet Union is, of course, not a member of NATO; and, while British, French and American forces would presumably remain in Germany under the framework of the NATO system, one must assume that those of the Soviet Union would be expected to depart. . . . So long, therefore, as this remains the Western position . . . I see little hope for any removal of the division of Germany at all —nor, by the same token, of the removal of the division of Europe.

Would the NATO guarantees of Germany's frontiers be considered as still standing if U.S. troops got out of Europe?

Mr. Kennan: Yes, and the atomic deterrent as still standing in our hands, and in English hands, and as operable, in the case of any attack on these continental countries.

Would the Soviet leaders really take their troops out of central Europe voluntarily, even at the risk of Hungarian-type revolts in the area?

Mr. Kennan: Well, all I can say is that . . . Mr. Bulganin has formally offered to Chancellor Adenauer to withdraw Soviet troops from the Eastern zone of Germany and from the other Warsaw Pact countries . . . in return for a withdrawal of American and British forces from the territory of other NATO countries. Now this may or may not be a proposition acceptable to us today, but it indicates that they're prepared to go quite far.

What about a place like Berlin—isn't there a danger that the Soviet Union could force us to take military action to defend our position in Berlin?

Mr. Kennan: That's just the trouble. May I point out that the Western position in Berlin is by no means a sound or safe one, and it is being rendered daily more uncertain by the ominous tendency of the Soviet government to thrust forward the East German regime as its spokesman in these matters. Moscow's purpose in this maneuver is . . . to place itself in a position where it can remain serenely aloof while the East German regime proceeds to make the Western position in the city an impossible one. . . .

Berlin is the one point where this can be "fuzzed" up to such a degree that we don't know whether it's Soviet aggression or not. Berlin's a place where they can theoretically force us to take the overt act.

Could we defend Berlin and a united and neutral Germany, with our troops and Soviet troops out of the country?

Mr. Kennan: Yes, because, of course, the city would immediately be restored then and would have a chance of life again . . . I think we could extend what amounts to a unilateral guarantee over [Germany], and I certainly should because I regard it as absolutely vital. Germany sits at the fulcrum of world power, as between the Russians and the Western world, and—what is your alternative to this? To keep it divided forever? That means Europe divided forever. . . .

Would the Germans agree to refrain from building up a big army—one that might threaten Europe as Hitler's did?

Mr. Kennan: I think the Germans would be rather glad to do it—it is, after all, we who pressed them into militarization, the initiative hasn't come from them . . . I think . . . National Socialism is deader today in Germany than was Bonapartism in France twelve years after the fall of Napoleon.

Suppose we leave a whole section of central Europe with nothing but a home guard—is this really a means of defense in our modern age?

Mr. Kennan: Yes, if you consider the alternatives. Suppose that there is a withdrawal from any of this area as there was, say, in Austria. What sort of defense are these countries going to have in the future? If they are going to have tactical atomic weapons, then the withdrawal has been no use at all, in my opinion, because the Russian Army . . . won't withdraw.

Your next possibility is that they remain armed with conventional forces on the World War II pattern. Those are not going to protect their frontiers against the sort of army that the Russians have got today, if that's what it comes to. That's not where their security lies; their security lies in the atomic deterrent. . . .

How can Western Europe get by with nothing but local forces?

Mr. Kennan: Switzerland has gotten by in two world wars, not because . . . she couldn't have been overrun but probably because it wouldn't have been worth while. . . . Now all I have in mind is that these countries cannot be defended at the frontier. Either they are defended in the air by the atomic weapon or they have to make occupation not worth while for someone else.

What does the West gain militarily by getting U.S. troops out of Germany?

Mr. Kennan: You must realize that, as a part of what I'm talking about, the Red Army would get back behind the borders of Poland. . . . Now, if the Red Army were to retire behind

Poland . . . a land attack on Western Europe would involve first the reoccupation of Poland and, believe me, there would be time from the Western standpoint to react to this.

Would all this be wrapped up in an agreement?

Mr. Kennan: I could see . . . an over-all European-security pact, embracing provisions governing the status of Germany, being signed by both sides—that is, by ourselves and the Russians. And yet the Atlantic Pact would continue undiminished and unaffected by it. . . . I assume this would take years to negotiate.

KENNAN'S VIEWS REJECTED [9]

I am told that the impression exists in Europe that the views expressed by Mr. George Kennan in his Reith lectures [a series of lectures broadcast by the British Broadcasting Corporation], particularly that a proposal should be made for the withdrawal of American, British and Russian troops from Europe, represent the views of the Democratic party in the United States. Mostly categorically they do not, as Mr. Kennan would, I am sure, agree. The opinions stated in the Reith lectures are not now made by Mr. Kennan for the first time. They were expounded by him within the Democratic Administration early in 1949, and rejected. They are today contrary to the expressed opinion of Democratic leaders in the Congress and outside of it.

Mr. Kennan can speak with authority in the field he knows —and a broad one it is—the field of Russian history and culture, and the attitudes of mind induced by the practice of Marxist-Leninist ideology.

Mr. Kennan has never, in my judgment, grasped the realities of power relationships, but takes a rather mystical attitude toward them. To Mr. Kennan there is no Soviet military threat in Europe.

If [he says] the armed forces of the United States and Britain were not present on the Continent, the problem of defense for the continental nations would be primarily one of the internal health and discipline of

[9] From text of statement by Dean Acheson, former Secretary of State, issued in New York by the American Council on Germany on January 11, 1958, as reprinted in *U.S. News & World Report.* 44:63. January 17, 1958.

the respective national societies, and of the manner in which they were organized to prevent the conquest and subjugation of their national life by unscrupulous and foreign-inspired minorities in their midst.

A desirable state of health and discipline would enable them to say to the Soviet Union that, while it had the power to overrun them, "not a single Communist or other person likely to perform your political business will become available to you for this purpose." Then follows this almost Messianic statement:

> I think I can give personal assurance that any country which is in a position to say to Moscow, not in so many words, but in that language of military posture and political behavior which the Russian Communists understand best of all, will have little need of foreign garrisons to assure its immunity from Soviet attack.

How can any man speak of a "personal assurance" to any such effect? On what does the guarantee rest, unless divine revelation? But, even in its terms, the assurance seems to contain its own refutation. In the present state of the distribution of power in this world, and in the light of the use made by the Russian Communist regime of its power to extend its authority, can one doubt that, were it not for the American connection, there would be more independent national life in Western Europe than there is in Eastern Europe?

Mr. Kennan's prescription for salvation by internal health and discipline within the national societies of Europe calls for a degree of wholesome purity which does not exist within any state I can think of. Not only that, but the normal and natural consequence of leaving Russian military power unopposable on the Continent would seem to mean a vast increase in the number of those Communists and other persons likely to perform Russian political business available to supplant those who ventured to oppose that business. The very withdrawal from the Continent of the Allies, whose presence alone permits Western Europe to withstand Soviet pressure, will make impossible the development of that national health and discipline which is supposed to make their presence unnecessary.

To speak, as Mr. Kennan did, of the alternative to American and British power in Europe as being "Soviet attack" is misleading. In many, perhaps in most, cases an attack by Soviet forces, faced with only token resistance, would not be necessary, as it was not in Czechoslovakia in 1948, or in Poland today. Soviet purposes could be accomplished by intimidation, with the lesson of Hungary in everyone's mind. Poland, by the way, might be the country which could come nearer than any in Europe to making the defiant declaration Mr. Kennan advocates. They know the Russians even better than Mr. Kennan does. But that does not free the Poles from Russian domination. It is idle to suppose that they would be more free if the power capable of opposing the Soviet Union withdrew from the Continent. . . .

Let me quote him again:

It cannot be stressed too often that NATO's real strength does not lie in the paper undertakings which underpin it; it lies—and will continue in any circumstances to lie—in the appreciation of the Western spiritual and cultural community. If this appreciation is there, NATO will not be weaker as a political reality, because it may be supplemented or replaced by other arrangements so far as Germany is concerned.

There are many things one might say about this. One is that the "other arrangements so far as Germany is concerned" would leave the military protection of Europe to massive nuclear retaliation, which is just where Mr. Kennan and all the rest of us do not want it to be. A second is that it indefinitely delays the day when nuclear weapons of all sorts might be canceled out and the guarantee of European security placed on Allied conventional forces. But perhaps the most pertinent statement for our present purpose is that, so long as we are giving personal assurances, I think I can give mine that Mr. Kennan's opinion is not shared by any responsible leader in the Democratic party in the United States.

IN FAVOR OF DISENGAGEMENT [10]

Our problem is not how to win the arms race, but how to end it.

[10] From "Is Disengagement in Europe Feasible?" by James P. Warburg, writer on American foreign policy. *Foreign Policy Bulletin.* 37:100+. March 15, 1958. Reprinted by permission.

But before there can be any real progress toward disarmament, there must be at least some disengagement, some unlocking of horns and, above all, a mutual recognition that neither side can hope to get more of what it wants than is obtainable through fair compromise.

The fatal pattern of the cold war, in which each side has stubbornly sought to obtain the unconditional surrender of the other instead of a fair compromise, was first set in Germany.

As long ago as 1949, I vainly endeavored to point out the fallacy of the European policy upon which the Truman administration was then embarking. . . .

Neutralization the Alternative

The alternative recommended was to recognize that neither we nor the Russians could reasonably hope to wrest control of a united Germany from the other; that a divided Germany would mean a divided and explosive Europe; and that the only way to reunite Germany would be to neutralize it. . . .

Whatever their ultimate motives, the Russians have, over the years, put forward repeated proposals for negotiation from which it is not too difficult to deduce, at least in part, what they would or would not be willing to do.

We know, for example, that the Russians will never agree to German reunification on terms permitting all of Germany to become a partner in the anti-Communist NATO alliance. Indeed, why should they? Yet this is precisely what we have been demanding at conference after conference for the past eight years.

We know that the Russians would like to get American forces out of Europe and that, for even a partial withdrawal, they would apparently pay a considerable price in the partial liberation of their satellites.

On November 17, 1956, the Soviet government proposed a withdrawal of all Western and Soviet forces from the European continent west of the Soviet frontier. The Arden House disarmament conference of December 1956 urged President Eisenhower to reply to the Soviet note with a counterproposal, suggesting, as the first step in a carefully phased mutual with-drawal, the retirement of Western forces behind the Rhine in exchange for a Soviet withdrawal behind the Oder and Neisse rivers. Two senators, one a Republican and the other a Demo-crat, took this proposal to the President. It was rejected, chiefly on the ground that Chancellor Konrad Adenauer, then about to run for reelection, would not approve of it.

During the disarmament talks at London early in 1957 Harold E. Stassen apparently attempted to revive the idea of a "thinned-out zone" in central Europe. These efforts were brought to a halt when, after Chancellor Adenauer's visit to Washington, Mr. Dulles flew to London in order to set Mr. Stassen upon what he conceived to be the right track.

On December 10, 1957, just before the NATO conference in Paris, Marshal Nikolai A. Bulganin wrote to Chancellor Adenauer, repeating the earlier Russian proposal and suggest-ing in addition the creation of a zone free of nuclear weapons to include not only East and West Germany, but Poland and Czechoslovakia as well. The latter idea had been originated by Poland's Foreign Minister Adam Rapacki.

Germany and Russia

Between his reelection in September 1957 and the NATO conference in December, Chancellor Adenauer found himself forced to make some concession to the prevailing current of German opinion, which flowed strongly toward the belief that, far from standing in the way of German reunification, a phased withdrawal of Soviet and Western forces from Germany might well create the only conditions in which reunification could take place. It was significant that, at the December 1957 NATO conference, it was he who led the revolt against the expressed American intention to ignore the Bulganin overtures.

At this NATO conference . . . [in] December an extraordi-nary thing happened. The final communiqué, of which Mr. Dulles was reported to be the chief author, contained the follow-ing paragraph:

At the Geneva conference of heads of government in July 1955 the Soviet leaders took a solemn commitment that "the unification of Germany by means of free elections shall be carried out in conformity with the national interests of the German people and the interests of European security." We call upon the Soviet government to honor this pledge.

President Eisenhower's NATO speech contained the same statement as to the alleged Soviet commitment, followed by this sentence:

Unhappily, that promise has been repudiated at the cost of the international confidence which the Soviet rulers profess to desire.

Now, according to responsible reporters present at the Geneva meeting in 1955, all that actually happened there with respect to Germany was that the chiefs of state issued a directive to the foreign ministers "to continue consideration" of the German question, stating their agreement that the matter of reunification by free elections should be settled "in conformity with the national interests of the German people and the interests of European security." The chiefs of state were unable to agree as to which of these two interests came first. Chalmers Roberts of the Washington *Post and Times Herald* recently commented in *The Reporter*: "Every newsman who was at Geneva, this writer included, knows that to be a fact. And so does Mr. Dulles."

Yet, the assertion that the Russians agreed at Geneva to unify Germany through free elections and later repudiated their solemn agreement was made by Mr. Dulles in a press conference, then in a speech at Chicago, and still later in an interview in London over the British Broadcasting Corporation just prior to the NATO conference. Finally, it found its way into the President's speech and, amazingly enough, into the NATO communiqué. It is now the foundation of our government's case against taking up the Bulganin proposals.

AGAINST DISENGAGEMENT [11]

If hydrogen bombs in sufficient number to destroy all life on the globe are stored in the arsenals of the United States, it

[11] From "Is Disengagement in Europe Feasible?" by George N. Shuster, president of Hunter College, New York City, author of books on Germany, and Land Commissioner for Bavaria in 1950-1951. *Foreign Policy Bulletin*. 37:101+. March 15, 1958. Reprinted by permission.

must be assumed that the Russians have, or soon will have, an equally ominous supply. The only way to forestall the suicide of the human race is to disarm. This means securing the adoption of three measures: multilateral supervision and control of all military installations; the formation of a neutral United Nations force to put the supervision and control into effect; and the systematic destruction, step by step, of all nuclear weapons other than the purely tactical ones. In my judgment it must be the primary concern of our foreign policy to bring about disarmament thus understood.

But what can possibly be gained at this juncture by weakening our military strength without obtaining a compensatory sacrifice of power from Moscow? Yet this is clearly what would happen were we to endorse George F. Kennan's proposal to bring about "disengagement in Europe" by assenting first of all to the neutralization of Germany. Note that Mr. Kennan's Reith lectures suggested this most tentatively and attached strings to the proposed bargain which may not have been taken into sufficient account in subsequent comment. Professor Hans Morgenthau of Chicago University and I twice discussed and publicly advocated a similar proposal during the years immediately following the war. Then Russian agreement to a neutral Europe might well have nipped the armament race in the bud and assured the freedom of Poland, Hungary and other countries. Unfortunately, there was never the slightest indication that such an agreement could be reached.

Russia Wants Vacuum

To what would Moscow be likely to assent today? Obviously it would like to create a military vacuum in central Europe, thus gaining advantages of immeasurable importance. But under such conditions the United States would have deprived itself, in the event of conflict, of a potentially very useful ally, Germany. The Russians would have secured such superiority of terrain for the use of tactical weapons that the only way of redressing the balance would be "massive retaliation" on our part—in other words, recourse to suicide. There is no discernible shred of evidence that, having obtained such a sacrifice from the West, the Kremlin would suddenly be eager to proceed with the only kind of disarmament that really counts. On this point the argument of Mr. Acheson seems to me wholly incontrovertible.

Consider, as a case in point, the Austrian peace treaty. Whatever may have induced the Russians, at long last, to sign this agreement, it was certainly not a loss of military advantage. By adding a long strip of neutral Austrian territory to an already neutral Switzerland, the Russians effectively prevented any accession of strength from Italy or the Mediterranean area to Western forces stationed in the north of Europe. If this was not a brilliant strategic move, it is difficult to conceive of one.

Returning to West Germany, it seems evident that a peace treaty which would involve the removal of American troops from Western Europe or, at the very least, place these troops at the gravest disadvantage by depriving them of tactical atomic weapons would be disastrous unless the political future of the whole of Germany had been democratically determined in advance. This the Russians have persistently vetoed. We have only to assume with virtual certainty that the withdrawal of Russian troops from the German Democratic Republic would be followed by an uprising to overthrow the government of Herr Walter Ulbricht in order to raise the fateful question, What would we do if the Russians then intervened with parachute troops and overran the "island" of Berlin? No doubt, nothing, save to welcome another group of refugees to Camp Kilmer.

A still more ominous consequence of "disengagement" as so far proposed would be a crushing blow to the forces which have been working hard for a united Europe. This is the only constructive idea which has grown out of the war. How can it be fostered if Germany is excluded from the NATO alliance, which is not only military but also economic and political in character? To consider the Rapacki "plan" from this point of view is to expose it as a device for weakening the West. It would compel recognition of the German Democratic Republic as a sovereign state and would at the same time, to all intents and purposes, disarm Western forces stationed in Germany.

To be sure, there are realistic ways of bringing about "European disengagement." These ways were spelled out in words of one syllable at the Berlin and Geneva conferences. If anyone can discern in the record any trace of Russian readiness to be realistic, well and good. But until then, daydreaming is merely a pastime.

A BRITISH LABOURITE VIEW [12]

Discussion on German reunification, neutralized zones and disengagement in Europe is often bedeviled by confusion over what exactly is being proposed. Critics of these ideas tend to group together several totally different plans and to denounce them all on the basis of arguments which apply only to some. . . .

For my part, I have never supported proposals for a neutralized, unarmed Germany on its own. On the contrary, when such ideas were being put forward during the great debate on German rearmament, I opposed them strongly. It seemed to me that they would have great disadvantages. They would have meant too big a sacrifice of territory by the West, since an evacuation by Russian troops of East Germany would be in no way comparable with the evacuation by Allied troops of the much larger area of Western Germany. Moreover, if Germany were to be unarmed, she might be too tempting a prize for a sudden, swift act of aggression, which would leave the West confronted with a *fait accompli*. Finally, at that time, it did really seem as though the creation of a united Germany would open the door to successful Communist subversion in the new state.

So far as I know, however, very few people nowadays put forward proposals of this kind. The argument about German reunification and disengagement has moved on to different ground. The change springs directly from the events of the autumn of 1956—revolt in Poland and revolution in Hungary, which altered the European situation in three ways. First, they threw a most vivid light on the weakness and extreme unpopularity of the Communist governments in the satellite states. It became clear that without the ultimate support of Russian troops

[12] From "Could We Accept a Neutralized Germany, United but Outside NATO?" article by Hugh Gaitskell, parliamentary leader of the British Labour Party. *Western World*. p41-4. July 1958. Reprinted by permission.

the Communist parties in Poland and Hungary could not remain in power. Thus, any idea that disengagement—involving the withdrawal of foreign forces from Germany—would lead to successful Communist subversion was illusory. On the contrary, in East Germany and the other satellite states it would be more likely to result in the overthrow of Communist regimes, while the threat of Communist revolution in Western Germany was obviously negligible.

Secondly, however, events in Poland and Hungary underlined the importance, from the point of view both of the West and of the Soviet Union, that steps should be taken to avert the highly dangerous situation inevitably resulting from any future outbreaks. It was bad enough during the Hungarian revolution when the West was faced with the choice between armed intervention—possibly leading to a third world war—and leaving the Hungarians to their fate, when with shame in our hearts we were obliged to follow the second course. But suppose, for example, a rising in East Germany occurred—a more violent and widespread version of the rioting in 1953—not next month but say in a year's time when a West German army was in existence? There would then be strong pressure in West Germany for their forces to intervene to help their fellow countrymen in the East. But if fighting started in this way between West Germany and the troops of the Soviet Union, how could NATO refrain from intervening too? There would thus be all the makings of a third world war. It is in the interests of the Russians as well as the West to try and prevent this from happening. Until recently the assumption of Western policy has been that the danger was planned Soviet aggression. Suez, Hungary—and perhaps Algeria—suggest that human passions are an even more likely source of conflict.

Balance of Security Needed

Thirdly, the events of 1956 indicated plainly how much trouble the satellite states were causing the Soviet government. If at one time the Russians had obtained any economic advantage from controlling these territories, it was not likely to continue. Economic concessions had now to be made to them. Moreover the development of nuclear weapons had made it rather less important that Russia should have a ring of satellite states well under its control. Thus—so it seemed—it might perhaps be satisfied with neighbors less closely attached to it for whom it had less responsibility, provided of course they were in no way actively hostile—and provided its security was improved in other ways as well.

It was with this background that some of us proceeded to try and work out a plan for disengagement—quite distinct from and not to be confused with earlier suggestions for an unarmed, neutralized Germany on its own.

It was clear that any plan, to have a chance of success, had to be based on certain principles. Most important of all, it must not alter the balance of security as between the Soviet bloc and NATO. For, if it did so, then the side which suffered disadvantage would be sure to reject the proposal. Thus there was little or no hope of Russia agreeing to German reunification so long as a reunited Germany was free to join and certainly would join NATO. But equally a plan involving the withdrawal of foreign troops from Germany alone could not be considered since it would give too much advantage to Russia as compared with the West. Compensation was necessary and might take the form of including in any disengagement zone at least Poland and Czechoslovakia and preferably Hungary as well.

The plan which we put forward has been expounded so often that it would not be necessary to repeat it, were it not for the danger of misunderstanding. I will, therefore, briefly summarize it as follows.

1. Foreign armed forces to be withdrawn from West Germany, East Germany, Poland, Czechoslovakia and Hungary. The time schedule of withdrawal to be negotiated although, no doubt, the process would be gradual.

2. Agreement on the level of conventional armed forces to be permitted to the countries in the zone, with full international control to insure that the agreement was being observed.

3. The reunification of Germany on the basis of free elections. We did not specify exactly how far the negotiations on this would have to be carried out by the great powers or at what

point negotiations might occur between the existing West and
East German governments. The framework of reunification
would certainly have to be agreed by the great powers, although
details might be left to direct discussions between the governments. The objection that this would involve recognition of the
East German Government would hardly apply if reunification had
already been agreed upon.

4. A security pact under which the frontiers of the states
within the zone would be guaranteed by these states themselves
and by the four great powers. We envisaged that a pact of this
kind would allow for radar screens to be set up on the western
and eastern frontiers and available for observers from all the
powers concerned.

5. Assuming that everything else had been agreed, Germany
to leave NATO and the three satellite states to leave the Warsaw
Pact.

Clearly a plan of this kind, if it could be agreed, would have
substantial advantages. In particular, it would have achieved the
reunification of Germany, without which, as has frankly been
acknowledged even by the opponents of such a plan, the danger
of war in Europe must continue.

Secondly, it would provide at least a pilot disarmament
scheme with full international controls. This might well be the
easiest way of making progress on disarmament, since, while the
Russians may at present object to effective controls within the
Soviet Union, it by no means follows that they would object to
such controls in central and eastern Europe. The existence of
such a scheme might itself, by creating greater confidence as to
the efficacy of controls, lead to a wider disarmament agreement.

Thirdly, it would certainly lead to a greater degree of freedom for the satellite states. It would be a mistake to assume that
they would automatically turn to the West, but they might evolve
in this way to the same status which—say—Finland or even
Austria at present enjoy.

There is one other advantage which might be expected to
emerge during the course of the negotiations. It is in practice
unlikely that any such plan could be agreed except in conjunction
with a final peace settlement. In other words, the negotiations

would almost certainly involve a treaty finally determining Germany's eastern frontier. Although German statesmen are naturally reticent on the subject, there is little doubt that they would be prepared to accept the existing frontier as permanent with perhaps minor adjustments if it was part of a treaty including German reunification. And from the point of view of Poland and the Soviet Union the final settlement of this problem might prove attractive in so far as German agreement had been obtained and the danger of a deliberate attempt to upset the status quo correspondingly reduced.

Conflicting Criticisms

It is, in the last analysis, no weakness of the plan that it has been attacked on opposite and conflicting grounds—that it is too dangerous for the West and, simultaneously, that the Soviet Union would not dream of accepting it. . . .

But of course both criticisms cannot be true. A plan which has real dangers for the West cannot also be to the grave disadvantage of the Russians and vice versa.

It is said that it is dangerous for the West because it would involve the break-up of NATO and the withdrawal of American troops across the Atlantic. There is no reason why this should be so. NATO existed before Western Germany was a member; and such American troops as continue to be required in Europe can be accommodated in France and the Low Countries and Britain. To be sure—if any such agreement on this were arrived at, and it would only be after long negotiations—one can reasonably hope that the extent of British and American forces necessary on the continent of Europe would be smaller. But we have always made it plain that in our opinion some British and American forces must remain.

Secondly, it is suggested that the "neutralization" of Germany will prove so attractive to other members of NATO that they will wish to follow suit and that consequently, the alliance will break up. This is to misunderstand the position of Germany under the proposed agreement. In one sense, it is to be neutralized, i.e., not to belong to any alliance. But this does not mean that it is "not involved" in any conflict. On the contrary it is abundantly clear that if there were to be a Soviet attack, Germany would be very heavily involved. There is, therefore, no question of it being able to avoid its geographical position and transform itself, so to speak, into another Switzerland or Sweden. Accordingly there is no reason why other countries should be particularly anxious to follow suit. As I have already pointed out, Germany will have its own national forces; and one need not necessarily assume that the burden of these will be much less than the burden carried by other members of NATO.

Will Germany still be part of the West?

This turns on the meaning of the phrase. There is no particular reason why its economic and cultural ties with the West should be weakened, though one certainly hopes that if the Iron Curtain crumbles to the extent that it would under this plan, then we shall not continue to speak of Europe as an area to the East of the Elbe. But, after all, Austria is part of the West today. Why should Germany not continue to be?

Finally, as I have already argued, the idea that the Soviet government would in these conditions be able to win over Germany to communism by stealth need not be taken seriously.

I do not believe, therefore, that the dangers for the West are real. Of course, it must be admitted that the withdrawal of Germany from NATO would, to some extent, weaken in absolute terms the military strength of the West but against this, the withdrawal of Russian forces to their own territory and some freeing of the satellite states from their present bondage is surely a most powerful compensation.

No doubt the argument that the Soviet Union would not accept a plan of this kind is more convincing. Indeed, I freely admit that in present circumstances, it seems unlikely. But I cannot agree that we should prejudge this issue. We none of us know for certain what Soviet policy will be. No doubt, at present, the Soviet government would reject the complete withdrawal of their forces from East Germany and the other satellite states; no doubt they insist that proposals for reunification are a matter for the two German governments though they are prepared to discuss at the "summit" a peace settlement. But Soviet policy can change rapidly and it may be that as time goes on they will come to see the advantages of a disengagement plan of this kind. In any case those of us who favor it may be pardoned if we look a little suspiciously at arguments that the Soviet must reject it from critics who would like the West to reject it too.

If, however, the prospect of any agreement on such an ambitious plan is, for the moment, rather bleak, it is worth considering whether something less far-reaching could not be considered. This would mean dropping the complete withdrawal of foreign troops and German reunification, together with the two consequential points, i.e., the security pact and the withdrawal of the countries concerned from NATO and the Warsaw Pact respectively. This would leave the possibility of some thinning out of foreign forces together with a local disarmament plan with full international controls over the national forces permitted by agreement to the territories in question.

It seems to me that there is a good prospect of agreement on these lines. The Polish government has recently put forward the Rapacki plan which involves a nuclear-free zone covering East and West Germany and also Poland and Czechoslovakia. It has also been intimated by the Poles that it might be possible to include in this plan control over conventional forces and a reduction in the foreign troops in the area in question. Thus the gap between the Rapacki plan and what I have suggested here is not large.

Admittedly, this would be only a small step forward, but it would be some advance; and any advance which helps to improve the present atmosphere and create rather more confidence and rather less suspicion seems to me worth while.

It may be said that the Russians are wholly unwilling to complete any agreement which does not give them a decided advantage. But must we assume that this will always be their attitude? If so, why did they agree to the Austrian treaty? Why has there not been more trouble in Indo-China? There are surely occasions when, very cautiously, but nevertheless quite definitely, they do seem prepared to make agreements—so long as these are not positively to their disadvantage—which lead to a relaxation of tension. I believe they might be prepared to do this in Europe today.

But even if this is not so, the case for putting forward positive suggestions of this kind remains as strong as ever. If the cold war is to continue and there is no hope of its declining intensity, we must continue to fight it, but we fight it best by ourselves advancing concrete, practical, reasonable proposals, which the Russians must either accept or else lose at least one propaganda battle. . . .

Finally, I must challenge the basic assumption of the critics of disengagement—that if we simply stand on our present position and wait, then everything will be all right in the end. We cannot take for granted that meanwhile the danger of war will be held in check or that the strength of NATO will be fully maintained. The morale of the West cannot be treated as something independent of our foreign policy. The negative line of the last four years has certainly been most unsuccessful in sustaining the faith of the democratic peoples. A positive policy aimed at dealing with what we believe to be the real causes of conflict is just as necessary for our security as the modern defense forces which —none of us would deny—are also required.

NEW BRITISH PROPOSALS [13]

The British government has prepared a three-point plan for assuring European security after reunification of Germany, Selwyn Lloyd, the Foreign Secretary, disclosed . . . [on December 4].

The Soviet proposal that West Berlin become a demilitarized free city was rejected by the Foreign Secretary. But the British government is ready for a "full" discussion with the Soviet Union about Germany's future and continental security, he said.

Mr. Lloyd emphasized that Britain still sought German unity through free elections throughout the country.

This concept and the whole idea of a Germany armed with nuclear weapons was bitterly assailed by Aneurin Bevan.

[13] From "Britain Proposes 3 Ways to Assure Europe's Security," by Drew Middleton, correspondent. New York *Times*. p 1. December 5, 1958. Reprinted by permission.

The Labour party's spokesman on foreign affairs told the House of Commons the free-elections formula for unity was a recipe for continued disunity. He described West Germany's position as one that allowed it to "blackmail" Poland and the Soviet Union.

Mr. Lloyd said Britain would try to meet Soviet fears of a united Germany.

The plan he presented follows:

1. Once Germany was united, Western troops would not move into what is now East Germany but would leave that area as a buffer between Poland and the Soviet Union and Western Europe.

2. Ground controls and aerial inspection would be established in as large an area of Europe as possible and perhaps beyond Europe to guard against surprise attack.

3. A system of agreed numbers and levels of arms would be set up in as large an area as possible. This would apply to both personnel and weapons, beginning with a system of inspection of existing armaments.

After having offered these as concrete proposals the British government would urge upon the United States, France and West Germany, Mr. Lloyd attacked the various plans for setting up a neutral zone in central Europe put forward by the East and the West.

Twice he became involved in heated exchanges with Mr. Bevan, whose fluency and aggressiveness contrasted sharply with Mr. Lloyd's rather halting defense of government policy.

The Rapacki plan, the eventual exclusion of nuclear armaments from central Europe, would discriminate against the West Germans and shift the strategic balance in favor of the Soviet Union's superior conventional forces, Mr. Lloyd contended.

Immediately Mr. Bevan was on his feet complaining that the system under which the United States controls nuclear warheads already had established "undesirable discrimination."

Mr. Lloyd plunged doggedly on into an explanation that in an era of intercontinental ballistic missiles and rockets a neutral zone was a mirage. It would be impossible to get the two sides so far apart that they could not fight, he said.

If this is so, Mr. Bevan interrupted, what is the good of leaving East Germany unoccupied by the Western forces, as Mr. Lloyd suggested.

Despite these forays from the Labour side, Mr. Lloyd's final argument against a neutral zone impressed the House.

Security in the Alliance

It was simply that the West was not strong enough in Europe to afford to change the balance of military security to its disadvantage, since without Atlantic alliance and United States troops in Europe there would be no security at all.

The Foreign Secretary maintained the government's line of cautious optimism toward the conference on a cessation of the tests of nuclear weapons now being held in Geneva. There has been some movement of the two sides closer together, he said.

Mr. Bevan made one of his strongest speeches since he assumed the role of Labour's spokesman in the international field. He echoed Mr. Lloyd's rejection of the Soviet proposals on Berlin, calling them "impractical" and "unacceptable."

Mr. Lloyd and Duncan Sandys, Minister of Defense who completed the government's case, saw West Germany as a source of Western strength. Mr. Bevan saw it in a more dangerous light.

The problems of Berlin, Germany and Europe are inextricably connected, the Labourite declared.

The government's complacency about Germany is quite as bad now as it was twenty years ago when the then Winston Churchill assailed it for allowing Germany to rearm, Mr. Bevan said. Sir Winston, sitting slumped in his corner, stared fixedly at his old opponent.

It seems that we have learned nothing at all, Mr. Bevan remarked.

Dr. Konrad Adenauer, West German Chancellor, was charged with a provocative statement that West Germany was not ready for a peace treaty. The West German leader may be delaying until his armed forces are stronger, Mr. Bevan suggested.

When will the time be ripe? Mr. Bevan asked: when all the German formations are established and when the Americans are there with nuclear warheads, ready to provide them should the need arise.

Labour's plan for Germany does not call for the nation, if reunited, to join the North Atlantic Treaty Organization. Mr. Bevan said the West would gain, rather than lose, through a disarmed Germany.

Mr. Bevan suggested that Britain rather than the United States become the leader of the free world since she had had more experience in international affairs.

In concluding the government's debate, Mr. Sandys said Soviet forces could not penetrate the present defenses of the West without incurring the risk of another world war. He said he doubted Moscow wanted to take such a risk.

But if the Atlantic pact forces were reduced and did not have nuclear weapons it would be comparatively easy for the Soviet forces to invade Western Europe hoping that the West would hesitate to start a world war to recover lost territory, Mr. Sandys remarked.

WHAT DOES RUSSIA WANT? [14]

The Bonn government is now certain that a diplomatic—if not physical—campaign against Berlin has begun. How will this campaign be waged, and for what purposes?

In the first place, practically nobody in Western Germany or in Berlin envisages a second, full-scale "Berlin blockade" of the 1947-1948 type. There are various reasons for assuming this. The Western powers have been quick to show that they are ready to withstand a second blockade; they have the planes with which to organize a second airlift, if necessary. West Berlin holds reserves of food and fuel sufficient for five or six months (in 1947, there were, practically speaking, no reserves at all). Furthermore, a full-scale blockade would deprive the East Germans of around 25 million marks a year (in hard currency) derived from the autobahn and canal tolls which they now impose on "alien" traffic, and would lead to the suspension of an interzonal trade which brings valuable heavy industrial products into Eastern

[14] From "Berlin Crisis: Tactics and Strategy," by Terence Prittie, Bonn correspondent of the *Manchester Guardian*. *Nation*. 187:424-6. December 6, 1958. Reprinted by permission.

Germany from the Ruhr. Above all, a full-scale blockade would carry heavy risks of war and refute the whole Soviet program of "normalizing" conditions in central Europe for the purpose of consolidating the status quo.

Both West German and Allied observers believe that what lies ahead in Berlin for the West is a "campaign of pinpricks." This could start with the withdrawal of the Soviet representative from the four-power "Air Safety Center"—the only four-power organization which has functioned in recent years. An East German could simply be installed in the place of the Russian, and the Western powers would have the choice of dealing with him or leaving the complicated problems of aircraft-control over Berlin to solve themselves.

Control of the air between Berlin and the West is a major East German objective. In the last ten years, 1.15 million East German refugees have been transported from West Berlin to Western Germany. This is roughly 40 per cent of the 3 million who have so far fled from East Germany. But since December 1957, when severe internal travel restrictions were imposed in East Germany, the proportion escaping via West Berlin has risen to around 80 per cent. And these have included an ever-increasing proportion of technicians, doctors, teachers—the people who can least be spared by a state which is running short of manpower and which is especially intended to be the "workshop" of the Eastern bloc.

A second pinprick could take the form of the removal of Soviet officials from the check-points on the Berlin-Hanover auto-bahn, along which all the military and official traffic of the three Western powers must move. The installation of East German officials at these check-points—and on the railway stations where Allied military trains are given clearance—would increase East German prestige, possibly force some kind of Western recognition of East German sovereignty and, in any event, weaken the Western position in Berlin psychologically.

At this stage, possible explanations of the Khrushchev *démarche* begin to emerge. The immediate Soviet objectives seem clear enough. They include Western recognition, or part-recognition, of the East German Republic; the weakening of Western prestige; the choking-off of the flow of East German refugees through Berlin to the West; the morale-boosting of the Ulbricht-Grotewohl regime in Berlin-Pankow; the gradual strangling of West Berlin independence and its eventual inclusion in the East German state. So obvious are these objectives that the Western powers can prepare counteraction to each of them. Secretary Dulles could publicly and dramatically repeat Allied guarantees of Berlin's independence—perhaps in Berlin itself.

West Berlin's Lord Mayor, Willy Brandt, could reiterate the steadfast determination of the Berliners to stand on their rights. (With the crisis at its height, Berliners made saucy jokes about the situation to each other; housewives refused to be panicked into buying non-perishable foodstuffs and fuel; the exchange rate of East marks to West marks remained steady at 4.35 East to 1 West.)

Ultimately, the Western powers could continue flying out East German refugees without the permission of either a Soviet or East German air-safety officer. For it is scarcely thinkable that Khrushchev would risk World War III by creating an "incident" in one of the air corridors from Berlin to the West. Ultimately, too, the Western powers could talk to East Germans without recognizing the East German regime—although this might turn out to be the first step down a slippery diplomacy slope.

But all of this has to do with obvious, short-term objectives. What is Khrushchev's long-range goal—the strategy behind the tactics? For one thing is certain: Soviet long-term planning is as much a feature of the current Berlin crisis as is the Soviet gift for improvised political maneuvering.

In this connection, one must survey Soviet policies in Germany since 1945 and out of the pattern, a great truth emerges. The Russians have been governed by two major lines of thought, each of which, at different times, has dominated Soviet policy. The first is unification: East Germany is a steppingstone to the Ruhr and the immensely greater material wealth of the Bonn Republic. In this context, West Germany is a *point d'appui* for the extension of Soviet influence to the borders of France and the Low Countries. The alternative concept is of an East Germany whose destiny is simply that of a Communist puppet state, an integral part of the satellite bloc.

The two policies have often run side by side without conflicting. But while Soviet readiness to take the bigger risk over Germany was evident in 1952 and again in 1955, the disciples of the lesser project—the consolidating of Germany as a member of the Communist bloc—have never ceased to work steadily towards their objective. The thoughts behind their labors have been that East Germany could become the most important industrial element in the whole Communist system; that its continued independent existence would guarantee the Oder-Neisse line with Poland and the finality of the ejection of 3 million Germans from the Czech Sudetenland; and that, once consolidated, it could still be used at a later date as a bastion from which to launch further political, economic and social pressure on Bonn.

But the biggest argument in favor of this concept is that only by keeping Germany divided can the satellite bloc be kept chained to the Soviet Union. For the Pole or Czech does not live who wants to see Germany reunified. At worst, reunification would mean to the smaller satellites the creation once again of a powerful and unpredictable neighbor; at best, it would mean a united Germany which would turn its face to the East, but would become a far more interesting factor than themselves to the Kremlin—and might even lead to territorial adjustments at their expense.

Has Khrushchev already written off any prospect of German reunification? Is he today paying only lip service to the idea? This is the most cogent question deriving from the Berlin crisis. The terms which the Soviet Premier has already set for German reunification are impossibly high: full recognition of East Germany, indefinite postponement of free elections in the whole of Germany, the elimination of "Fascists and militarists" from the Federal Republic, the military neutralization of Germany and (admittedly by inference only) the withdrawal of all American armed forces from the European continent. Does Khrushchev **really think that these terms** have any chance of success? Or were they always intended to make Western acceptance impossible, so that the satellite bloc can be consolidated and the Soviet Union can sit back for a decade before making the next move westward?

AN OFFICIAL WEST GERMAN VIEW [15]

For almost two decades—from 1921 to 1940—the Soviet Union was a relatively stable factor in international politics, with unchanged territorial dimensions. Then, however, there was an abrupt change: the Baltic States were, to all intents and purposes, annexed (August 1940), Finnish territory was conquered by force of arms, Poland was shared with Hitler. After World War II, this territorial expansion continued: in addition to the Baltic, Finnish and Polish areas, German, Czechoslovakian, Rumanian and Japanese territories were annexed. Moreover, a new form of expansion began—the extension of political power through the establishment of a satellite realm in Eastern Europe. This was done by bringing about revolutions in various countries up till then independent (Poland, Hungary, Yugoslavia, Rumania, Bulgaria, Albania), turning them into so-called People's Democracies.

When, in addition, this revolutionary process took hold of Czechoslovakia, threatened to disintegrate Greece, and, with the Berlin blockade, put to the test the possibilities of conquering Germany, the Western world finally recognized that Europe could be saved from further expansion of this kind only by determined and drastic measures. The result of this recognition was the policy of containment, which found expression in the proclamation of the Marshall Plan and the Truman Doctrine (1947), the organization of the Berlin airlift (1948-1949), the conclusion of the North Atlantic Pact (1949), and the decision to arm the German Federal Republic (1950).

Communism has adjusted to the situation which these measures created. For the last several years, the Soviet Union has, neither in Europe nor elsewhere, undertaken territorial expansion by manifest force of arms. But Communist propaganda has more and more been making use of a formula which, at first glance, seems to indicate that a policy of stability and non-expansion is at work—the formula advocating maintenance of the status quo by mutual agreement between East and West. Upon closer examination, it emerges, however, that this formula is quite com-

[15] From "Implications of Disengagement," by Professor Wilhelm Grewe, German Ambassador to the United States. *The Bulletin* (issued by the Press and Information Office of the German Federal Government). 6:1-3. September 2, 1958.

patible with the long-range goals of world communism, for it is always complemented by the statement that in future the controversy between the two great ideological and political power systems should take place in the form of "peaceful competition."

"Peaceful Coexistence"

At last year's meeting of the Supreme Soviet—on February 12, 1957—it was plainly stated for all to hear that peaceful coexistence "is strife—political strife, economic strife, ideological strife." By peaceful coexistence the Soviets do not mean renunciation of world revolution; on the contrary, the Communist party's Moscow Declaration of November 1957, emphasized that "the major feature of our epoch is the process of transition from capitalism to communism." True, the laboring class would, it was explained, strive to carry out the revolution by peaceful means, seizing governmental power without civil war, keeping, however, the possibility of a non-peaceful transition in mind, in case the "exploiting classes" should use force against the people instead of voluntarily relinquishing power.

"Status Quo"

What, then, does the phrase "status quo" mean when Khrushchev uses it today? It means that the West should reconcile itself to the subjugation of Eastern Europe to Communist dictatorship, to the partitioning of Germany, to the isolation of Berlin; it means that Moscow intends to undertake no direct military conquests but reserves to itself the right to gain new territory by other means, be it with the help of Communist parties in Western Europe (not very promising at the moment), or be it in Africa and Asia (where Moscow calculates that the chances are better).

"Disengagement"

At this very moment the question is being raised in the West whether or not the time has come to replace the policy of containment with a policy of disengagement.

Just what is meant by disengagement and what purpose is it supposed to serve? There are many definitions and explanations in answer to these questions, such as that the large military blocs should be moved apart, a neutral belt being established between them in order to eliminate points of friction, and their adjacent fields be made strategically uninteresting, removed from the great powers' sphere of military rivalry.

Among the concrete disengagement proposals which have been made there are two in the foreground: the proposal of an atom-free zone in central Europe (Rapacki plan) and the more comprehensive proposal of bilateral withdrawal from central and eastern Europe of the great powers' military forces which are stationed on foreign soil. In the form in which at present they are usually recommended, both these proposals are extremely dangerous, even though they do contain certain positive elements and logical thoughts which it might in due time and in a broader connection be possible to apply.

Rapacki Plan

Every military expert, whether in the West or the East, knows that by a total prohibition of atomic weapons in central Europe, as is recommended in the Rapacki plan, the position of the American, British and Canadian armed forces in Germany would be made untenable, sooner or later compelling them to withdraw. This would happen not only because of the inadequacy of their means of defense but because the entire armed forces of the countries in question have long since begun to be adjusted to the methods of atomic warfare, so that they cannot in Germany maintain troops which, in training, equipment and organization, stand still at an outdated stage of military techniques. Thus, the Rapacki plan can only be taken as a curtain-raiser of a "greater solution," of troop withdrawal—disengagement in the widest sense—and that is why an evaluation of the Rapacki plan will be positive or negative all in accordance with one's evaluation of this "greater solution."

"Greater Solution"

Nobody can deny that some day the solution of Europe's great political issues might possibly require a bilateral withdrawal of troops. But decisive for the contemplation of such a solution will be when and under what conditions it is undertaken. In this respect the plans thus far discussed cannot but arouse strong misgivings.

To a large extent they misjudge or neglect the difficult question of the "equability" of troop withdrawal by both sides. It is not true that the withdrawal of the Red Army to within the boundaries of the Soviet Union and the withdrawal of the Anglo-American armed forces from the European Continent could even begin to reestablish the kind of balance of political power which existed before the war. Whoever believes it could is ignoring the last two decades' enormous changes in the power potential of the European peoples. If such a withdrawal were made today or tomorrow it would cause a definite shift in Europe's power balance, not only unfavorable to the West but bound to endanger European freedom.

The Question of Guarantees

Not even a halfway satisfactory answer has as yet been given to the most important question which the withdrawal of the Red Army would pose—the question of effective guarantee against this Army's return, sooner or later, to the places where it was previously stationed. Put this way, it becomes clear that the proposal of bilateral troop withdrawal is unfortunately a great deal more problematical than many champions of disengagement would have it. For if the purpose of troop withdrawal is to separate the armed forces of the great powers in possession of atomic weapons, in order to prevent conflict between them, the following question poses itself: might not the realization of this proposal bring in its train situations that would, more than any previous ones, evoke the acute danger of a clash? We have seen it happen before, in Korea, that "disengagement" quickly led to war.

Possible Consequences

There is no longer any doubt but that a withdrawal of the Red Army from Eastern Europe would inevitably lead to a revolutionary situation in what are today the satellite countries. Not one of the Communist regimes could persist without Soviet military backing, least of all the Ulbricht-Grotewohl regime in the Soviet zone of Germany. Most likely there would be a repetition of the events which took place on June 17, 1953, in Berlin, or during November, 1956, in Budapest. What then? Is it to be expected that the Soviets would passively look on? Of course not; they could not afford inactivity, since the violent overthrow of a Communist regime through spontaneous revolt of the people would be an event to shake the foundations of their rule, not only in all subjugated countries but possibly also in their own.

The Basis of Future Disengagement

One day, perhaps, it may be possible to put Europe entirely on its own feet again and do without oversea troops stationed here. But the indispensable prerequisite of this, the strengthening of Europe, will certainly be made impossible by neutralizing and demilitarizing Germany—be it Germany alone or Germany as part of a central European belt—or by effectively preventing Germany in any other way from establishing a military force congruent with its capacity to do so. Those who champion restrictions of this sort do not promote but destroy what could be the basis of a possible, future disengagement.

"Let Us Be Careful . . ."

Discernment of the consequences which an insufficiently safeguarded transition from containment to disengagement might have is bound to lead to the apprehension that disengagement might gradually, almost imperceptibly, slip into appeasement. Many who today champion disengagement would protest against being associated with a policy of appeasement. Subjectively, no doubt, their reaction would be justified, but one must be allowed to call attention to certain objective consequences and to pose the question: Where is disengagement supposed to lead—what will be the next step?

Let us be careful about assuming that atom-free or militarily thinned-out belts would definitely minimize the danger of war. There is also the opposite possibility. In our day, there is small chance of war being caused by incidents occurring between two armies stationed in close proximity to each other. The Korean War broke out not because of the presence of U.S. armed forces in South Korea but because of their withdrawal. More dangerous, therefore, than the geographical proximity of the respective armed forces seems to be the disproportion of military strength in the border areas between East and West. This should be borne in mind by those who propose atom-free or otherwise militarily thinned-out zones or plan still other kinds of disengagement projects.

BERLIN: A CONSTRUCTIVE RESPONSE [16]

The note of the United States, Britain, and France to the Soviet Union in reply to the latter's proposals on Berlin is a model of brevity and compactness. It is also an example of openminded thinking which should make an impression in some neutral countries if not also in Moscow.

The note expresses a willingness to discuss the German problem in a broad rather than limited framework and to do this in the presence of advisers who could represent the elected West German government and the Communist puppet regime of East Germany.

This represents a dual concession on the part of the Western powers—a flexibility for which they should receive credit. In the first place, it extends a kind of semirecognition to the Soviet-supported East German government, which Moscow has insisted must be dealt with in any reunification of Germany. Second, it opens a door to the discussion of proposals for a neutralization of Germany, a disengagement of forces in central

[16] Editorial. *Christian Science Monitor.* February 17, 1959. p 12. Reprinted by permission.

Europe, a ban on nuclear weapons there, and a possible European security system.

These are subjects on which Premier Khrushchev and Foreign Minister Gromyko have placed much emphasis. They have advocated a disarmed West Berlin and supported the Polish Rapacki plan for a denuclearized zone.

At the same time they have blown hot and cold about the question of free elections for East Germany. They have hinted they might not object to these, but have proved obdurate when there was the faintest practical prospect of a test of opinion which could only pull down the East German Communist façade.

Now, the point can properly be made that if the West is willing to talk about phases of the German problem on which Moscow wants to play propaganda themes, then Soviet diplomacy should be willing also to have the question raised by what other methods—if not by free elections—a conscionable and workable reunification of Germany can be brought about.

The Western note proposes that a conference of foreign ministers of the Soviet Union, Britain, France, and the United States be held to "deal with the problem of Germany in all its aspects and implications." While no date is set, it is thought possible that this meeting could take place in late April or early May.

Such a timing would come within the six months Moscow allowed when it vowed to turn over Soviet authority in East Germany to the puppet government there. If Moscow is co-operative, the talks could lead to a summit meeting such as Mr. Khrushchev has desired, to include himself and President Eisenhower.

The three-power counterproposal reflects great credit on its chief architect, Secretary of State Dulles, who has brought together the views of Mr. Eisenhower, Prime Minister Macmillan, President de Gaulle, and Chancellor Adenauer. The note avoids polemics or argument of the issues, and thereby makes perhaps as great a contribution as any to an atmosphere for negotiation.

BIBLIOGRAPHY

An asterisk (*) preceding a reference indicates that the article or a part of it has been reprinted in this book.

BOOKS AND PAMPHLETS

Acheson, Dean. Power and diplomacy. 137p. Harvard University Press. Cambridge, Mass. '58.

Adenauer, Konrad. World indivisible: with liberty and justice for all; tr. by Richard and Clara Winston. 128p. Harper & Bros. New York. '55.

Alexander, Edgar. Adenauer and the new Germany. 300p. Farrar, Straus & Cudahy. New York. '57.

Barraclough, Geoffrey. Origins of modern Germany. 481p. Macmillan Co. New York. '48.

Bathurst, M. E. and Simpson, J. L. Germany and the North Atlantic community. 217p. Frederick A. Praeger. New York. '56.

Bolles, Blair. Big change in Europe. 527p. W. W. Norton & Co. New York. 1958.

Clay, L. D. Decision in Germany. 83p. Doubleday & Co. Garden City, N.Y. '50.

Colegrove, Kenneth. Democracy versus communism. 424p. D. Van Nostrand Co. Princeton, N.J. '57.

*Conant, J. B. Federal Republic of Germany, our new ally; speech delivered as Gideon D. Seymour Memorial Lecture, University of Minnesota, February 24, 1957. 20p. University of Minnesota Press. Minneapolis. '57.

Conant, J. B. Germany and freedom: a personal appraisal. 117p. Harvard University Press. Cambridge, Mass. '58.

Connell, Brian. Watcher on the Rhine, an appraisal of Germany today. 320p. William Morrow & Co. New York. '57.

Davison, W. P. Berlin blockade. 423p. Princeton University Press. Princeton, N.J. '58.

Deutsch, H. C. Our changing German problems. 64p. Science Research Associates. Chicago. '56.

Erhard, Ludwig. Prosperity through competition; tr. by E. T. Roberts and J. B. Wood. 272p. Frederick A. Praeger. New York. '58.

Finletter, T. K. Foreign policy: the next phase. 208p. Harper & Bros. New York. '57.

German Federal Government. Press and Information Office. Facts on Germany. 16p. Press Office of the German Embassy. 1742 R St. Washington 9, D.C. '57.

Haines, C. G. ed. European integration. 310p. Johns Hopkins Press. Baltimore. '57.

Haines, C. G. What future for Europe? (Headline Series no 124) 62p. Foreign Policy Association. New York. '57.

Hall, W. P. Europe in the twentieth century. 482p. Appleton-Century-Crofts. New York. '57.

Hayes, C. J. H. Contemporary Europe since 1870. 835p. Macmillan Co. New York. '58.

Hiscocks, Richard. Democracy in Western Germany. 324p. Oxford University Press. New York. '57.

Horne, Alistair. Return to power: a report on the new Germany. 415p. Frederick A. Praeger. New York. '56.

Jackson, R. H. Case against the Nazi war criminals. 216p. Alfred A. Knopf. '46.

Kennan, G. F. Russia, the atom and the West. 116p. Harper & Bros. New York. '57.

Kissinger, H. A. Nuclear weapons and foreign policy. 463p. Harper & Bros. New York. '57.

Klemperer, Klemens von. Germany's new conservatism: its history and dilemma in the twentieth century. 250p. Princeton University Press. Princeton, N.J. '57.

Kohn, Hans. German history: some new German views. 224p. Beacon Press. Boston. '54.

*Kohn, Hans. West Germany: new era for German people. (Headline Series no 131) 62p. Foreign Policy Association. New York. Sept.-Oct. '58.

Krieger, Leonard. German idea of freedom: history of a political tradition. 540p. Harcourt, Brace and Co. New York. '57.

Litchfield, E. H. Governing postwar Germany. 661p. Cornell University Press. Ithaca, N.Y. '53.

Lochner, L. P. Tycoons and tyrants: German history from Hitler to Adenauer. 304p. Henry Regnery Co. Chicago. '54.

Montgomery, J. D. Forced to be free: the artificial revolution in Germany and Japan. 209p. University of Chicago Press. Chicago. '57.

Moore, B. T. NATO and the future of Europe. (Council on Foreign Relations Publication) 263p. Harper & Bros. New York. '58.

Organisation for European Economic Co-operation. Economic conditions in the Federal Republic of Germany. 15p. OEEC Mission, Publications Office. 1346 Connecticut Ave. Washington 6, D.C. '57.

Pinson, K. S. Modern Germany: its history and civilization. 637p. Macmillan Co. New York. '54.

Speier, Hans. German rearmament and atomic war: the views of German military and political leaders. 272p. Row, Peterson & Co. Evanston, Ill. '57.

Speier, Hans and Davison, W. P. eds. West German leadership and foreign policies. 323p. Row, Peterson & Co. Evanston, Ill. '57.

Taylor, A. J. Course of German History. 230p. Coward-McCann. New York. '46.

Taylor, Telford. March of conquest. 460p. Simon and Schuster. New York. '58.

Thayer, C. W. Unquiet Germans. 275p. Harper & Bros. New York. '57.

*United States. Department of State. Soviet note on Berlin: an analysis. (Department of State Publication 6757) 53p. Supt. of Docs. Washington 25, D.C. '59.
    Reprinted in this book: Excerpts appearing in the New York Times. p4. Ja.8, '59.

Wallich, H. C. Mainsprings of the German revival. 401p. Yale University Press. New Haven, Conn. '55.

Weymar, Paul. Adenauer; his authorized biography; tr. by Peter de Mendelssohn. 509p. E. P. Dutton & Co. New York. '57.

Wiskemann, Elizabeth. Germany's Eastern neighbours. 309p. Oxford University Press. New York. '56.

Wright, D. M. Post-war West German and U. K. recovery. 25p. American Enterprise Association. 1012 14th St. Washington 5, D.C. '57.

Zink, Harold. United States in Germany, 1944-1955. 374p. D. Van Nostrand Co. Princeton, N.J. '57.

Zurcher, A. J. Struggle to unite Europe, 1940-1958. 254p. New York University Press. New York. '58.

PERIODICALS

America. 99:584+. S. 6, '58. Silent revolt. Franz Schneider.

American Political Science Review. 52:513-30. Je. '58. Government, administration, and politics in West Germany: a selected bibliography. J. B. Mason.

Annals of the American Academy of Political and Social Science. 312: 77-83. Jl. '57. Soviet Union and German rearmament. F. L. Schuman.

Annals of the American Academy of Political and Social Science. 312: 84-8. Jl. '57. German defense contribution. H. L. Krekeler.

Annals of the American Academy of Political and Social Science. 317: 153-63. My. '58. East Europe, Germany and the West. J. C. Campbell.

*Atlantic Monthly. 199:99-190. Mr. '57. Perspective of Germany; an Atlantic supplement assembled by Intercultural Publications Inc.
    Reprinted in this book: German character and history. Theodor Heuss (tr. by Richard and Clara Winston). p 103-9; Germany today and tomorrow. Konrad Adenauer (tr. by Rudolf Ernst). p 110-12.
    Also separate: 94p. Intercultural Publications Inc. 60 E. 42d St. New York 17. '57.

Atlantic Monthly. 200:49-54. S. '57. Konrad Adenauer. Terence Prittie.

*Atlantic Monthly. 200:12+. D. '57. Atlantic report on the world today—Germany.

*Atlantic Monthly. 201:6+. Ja. '58. Atlantic report on the world today —Berlin.

Atlantic Monthly. 202:12-15. Jl. '58. Atlantic report on the world today—Bonn.

Atlantic Monthly. 202:37-41. S. '58. New Europe. P.-H. Spaak.

Atlantic Monthly. 202:16+. O. '58. Atlantic report on the world today —East Germany.

Bulletin (Press and Information Office of the German Federal Government). 6:7-8. Ag. 12, '58. Industrial pattern.

*Bulletin (Press and Information Office of the German Federal Government). 6:1-3, S. 2, '58. Implications of disengagement. Wilhelm Grewe.

*Bulletin (Press and Information Office of the German Federal Government). 6:5. S. 23, '58. 1958 CDU Convention.

*Bulletin (Press and Information Office of the German Federal Government). 6:2+. O. 7, '58. We are one nation and wish to remain so! Ernst Lemmer.

*Bulletin (Press and Information Office of the German Federal Government). 6:4-5. N. 4, '58. A Briton reports. Peter Kirk.

*Business Week. p65. Mr. 29, '58. Bank gets credit for German revival.

Catholic World. 185:186-92. Je. '57. Sinister Germany? H. C. Graef.

Catholic World. 186:324-5. F. '58. Kennan and Russian treachery. J. B. Sheerin.

Catholic World. 186:333-7. F. '58. Where Kennan is wrong. J. J. Hanlin.

Christian Century. 75:132-3. Ja. 29, '58. Pastor Niemöller states his case. Robert Wuliger.

Christian Science Monitor. p9. F. 5, '59. Konrad Adenauer: durable, single-purposed. W. H. Stringer.

*Christian Science Monitor. p 12. F. 17, '59. Berlin: a constructive response.

Commentary. 19:137-46. F. '55. Fragmented people that is Germany. F. R. Stern.

Commentary. 19:406-10. Ap. '55. Nazi era. Manfred Wolfson.

Commentary. 23:222-30. Mr. '57. Program for a European settlement. Hugh Seton-Watson.

Commonweal. 65:657-9. Mr. 29, '57. Pilgrimage to Dachau. M. H. Philipson.

Contemporary Review. 192:98-101. Ag. '57. Israel and the German Federal Republic.

Current History. 28:193-250. Ap. '55. Germany's foreign policy.
    Entire issue.

Current History. 30:193-239. Ap. '56. Report on Germany.
    Entire issue.

Current History. 34:33-6. Ja. '58. Russian control of east-central Europe. R. F. Byrnes.

Economist. 179:775-6. My. 26, '56. German eyes on developing nations.

*Economist. 187:125-6. Ap. 12, '58. Look of permanence.

*Economist. 187:323-4. Ap. 26, '58. Dogma and practice.

Foreign Affairs. 35:432-40. Ap. '57. German paradoxes. Claus Jacobi.

Foreign Affairs. 36:460-71. Ap. '58. New initiatives for a new age: German view. W. W. Schütz.

Foreign Affairs. 36:611-17. Jl. '58. Germany's economic goals. Ludwig Erhard.

Foreign Affairs. 37:187-210. Ja. '59. Disengagement revisited. G. F. Kennan.

*Foreign Policy Bulletin. 37:25-6. N. 1, '57. Adenauer's victory: an advance for democracy? L. W. Holborn.

*Foreign Policy Bulletin. 37:100+. Mr. 15, '58. Is disengagement in Europe feasible? J. P. Warburg; G. N. Shuster.

Foreign Policy Bulletin. 37:124+. My. 1, '58. U.S. foreign policy in a changing world. V. M. Dean.

Fortune. 56:136-41+. D. '57. Europe's new age of abundance. G. H. Burck and S. S. Parker.

Journal of International Affairs. 12, no 1:82-9. Ja. '58. Germany and the Western alliance. Konrad Adenauer.

Look. 21:84-5. S. 3, '57. Adenauer talks; interview. Konrad Adenauer.

Monthly Review (Federal Reserve Bank of New York). 40:177-80. D. '58. Recent economic developments in West Germany.

Nation. 182:365. Ap. 28, '56. Germany: new myths for old. F. L. Schuman.

Nation. 185:133. S. 14, '57. Unquiet flows the Elbe. F. L. Schuman.

*Nation. 187:424-6. D. 6, '58. Berlin crisis: tactics and strategy. Terence Prittie.

New Republic. 136:12-15. Mr. 11, '57. Time-bomb ticks in East Germany. Sebastian Haffner.

New Republic. 137:8. Ag. 26, '57. Khrushchev opts for a divided Germany.

New Republic. 138:13-15. F. 24, '58. Germany: four proposals and a dissent to George Kennan. Perry Laukhuff.

New Statesman. 54:243. Ag. 31, '57. Two Germanys. R. H. S. Crossman.

*New York Herald Tribune. Sec. 2, p4. N. 2, '58. Red "corvee" in East Germany.

*New York Herald Tribune. p 1. N. 10, '58. Crisis welcome to East Germans. Gaston Coblentz.

New York Herald Tribune. p22. D. 2, '58. From Berlin to Germany. Walter Lippmann.

New York Herald Tribune. p 16. Ja. 15, '59. U.S. position on German unity; editorial.

*New York Times. p49. Ja. 7, '58. Bonn's strength spreads in world. M. S. Handler.

*New York Times. p4. My. 3, '58. Bonn would drop anti-cartel law. M. S. Handler.

*New York Times. p 18. My. 3, '58. West Germany and nuclear arms. C. L. Sulzberger.

*New York Times. p 14. Ag. 10, '58. Nazi data bared by unit in Munich. Harry Gilroy.

*New York Times. p25. Ag. 24, '58. Ex-Nazi officials vex red Germany. Harry Gilroy.

*New York Times. p5. N. 5, '58. Rapacki proposes 2-stage plan for atom ban in Central Europe.

*New York Times. p E5. N. 23, '58. Large goals set in East Germany. Sydney Gruson.

*New York Times. p 1+. N. 28, '58. Moscow proposes West Berlin be free city. Max Frankel.

New York Times. p 10. N. 28, '58. U.S. statement on Berlin; text of State Department statement of November 27, 1958.

*New York Times. p E3. N. 30, '58. Khrushchev's move offers challenge to U.S. Drew Middleton.

*New York Times. p E5. N. 30, '58. Basic documents behind the struggle for Germany and Berlin. Harry Schwartz.

*New York Times. p E5. N. 30, '58. Germany: the opposing views. A. J. Olsen.

New York Times. p4. D. 1. Berlin—I; p4. D. 2, '58. Berlin—II. H. W. Baldwin.

*New York Times. p 1. D. 5, '58. Britain proposes 3 ways to assure Europe's security. Drew Middleton.

*New York Times. p E4. D. 7, '58. East Germany ruled by an ersatz regime. A. J. Olsen.

New York Times. p E6. Ja. 25, '59. Ruhr industry back to pre-war structure. A. J. Olsen.

New York Times. p30. Ja. 28, '59. Soviet challenge and Western response; editorial.

New York Times. p E5. F. 1, '59. Europeans still fear revival of Germany. Sydney Gruson.

New York Times. p 1+. F. 11, '59. Tactics on Berlin detailed by West; unity is achieved. D. A. Schmidt.

New York Times. p 1-2, 3. F. 13, '59. Mansfield urges that two Germanys fix Berlin unity; excerpts from speech by Senator Mike Mansfield to the U.S. Senate, February 12, 1959.

New York Times Magazine. p20+. Ap. 6, '58. Post-war tide has run out. M. S. Handler.

*New York Times Magazine. p 14-15+. My. 11, '58. First hundred days of the Hitler nightmare. F. E. Hirsch.

New York Times Magazine. p 10+. Ja. 4, '59. 'Der Alte' at 83; symbol of a new Germany. Flora Lewis.

New York Times Magazine. p 15+. F. 1, '59. Moscow's no. 1 man in Germany. Flora Lewis.

News From Germany (Executive Committee of the Social Democratic Party of Germany). 11:1-3. Jl. '57. Danger of atomic armament. Fritz Erler.

News From Germany (Executive Committee of the Social Democratic Party of Germany). 11:1-4. Jl. '57. Election program of the Social Democratic Party of Germany.

News From Germany (Executive Committee of the Social Democratic Party of Germany). 11:1. N. '57. Free Berlin and its mission. Willy Brandt.

*News From Germany (Executive Committee of the Social Democratic Party of Germany). 11:1-3. D. '57. Tasks of the third Bundestag. Erich Ollenhauer.

Newsweek. 50:47. D. 9, '57. Calling Russia's hand.

Newsweek. 51:42. Je. 2, '58. Socialist revolt.

Newsweek. 51:94+. Je. 23, '58. Up from the debris. Franz Spelman.

Political Science Quarterly. 73:1-27. Mr. '58. Adenauer and a crisis in Weimar democracy. F. R. Stern.

Population Index. 24:3-21. Ja. '58. Economic and demographic developments in Western Germany. Dudley Kirk.

Reader's Digest. 70:148-53. Je. '57. Germany bounces back. Lin Root.

Reader's Digest. 72:113-16. Ja. '58. NATO's German general. André Visson.

Reader's Digest. 73:117-20. S. '58. New watch on the Rhine. Corey Ford and James Perkins.

Reporter. 18:15-18. Ap. 3, '58. Eighteen German physicists say there must be an end. Robert Jungk.

Rotarian. 92:8-10+. Ap. '58. Germany's intellectual earthquake. Leland Stowe.

Saturday Evening Post. 229:28-9+. Je. 1, '57. Will East Germany blow again? J. P. O'Donnell.

Saturday Evening Post. 230:10+. My. 3, '58. Germany's free economy outpaces Socialist rivals.

Science. 125:1136. Je. 7, '57. Teacher shortage in West Germany.

Senior Scholastic. 70:9-12. Mr. 8, '57. Germany faces the crossroads.

*Swiss Review of World Affairs. 8:6-8. Ag. '58. "Atomic death" in Western Germany. Fred Luchsinger.

Swiss Review of World Affairs. 8:3-5. D. '58. Reunification: a risky topic of debate in Germany. Fred Luchsinger.

Time. 71:24. Mr. 10, '58. Crackup, crackdown.

Time. 71:17. Mr. 31, '58. NATO or disengagement.

Time. 71:24. Ap. 21, '58. Benevolent concession; Soviet—West German trade.

U.S. News & World Report. 42:106-8. My. 3, '57. A-bombs for Germany: declaration of scientists, reply by Adenauer and joint communiqué.

U.S. News & World Report. 42:62-3. Je. 7, '57. We demand reunion with East Germans; address to Senate, May 28, 1957. Konrad Adenauer.
    Same. United States Department of State Bulletin. 36:958-60. Je. 17, '57; *same with title* Freedom, peace, unity. Vital Speeches of the Day. 23:514-15. Je. 15, '57.

U.S. News & World Report. 42:32-6. Je. 14, '57. Story Khrushchev didn't tell; West and East Berlin.

U.S. News & World Report. 43:39-40. Jl. 19, '57. Close-up of Communist failures. K. Lachmann.

U.S. News & World Report. 43:30-2. Ag 2, '57. How to have a boom without a price rise; interview with Ludwig Erhard.

*U.S. News & World Report. 43:48+. S. 20, '57. From rubble to riches in 12 years.

*U.S. News & World Report. 44:69-70+. Ja. 10, '58. Kennan ideas that are stirring up Europe.
    Excerpts from George F. Kennan's Reith lectures broadcast by the British Broadcasting Corporation.

*U.S. News & World Report. 44:63. Ja. 17, '58. Acheson rejects Kennan plan; excerpts from statement. Dean Acheson.

U.S. News & World Report. 44:100-2. Mr. 21, '58. Free enterprise vs. socialism.

U.S. News & World Report. 44:88-92. Ap. 25, '58. Dean Acheson warns: danger in summit talks; address.

*U.S. News & World Report. 45:85+. S. 26, '58. 12 years under communism and still they flee.

*U.S. News & World Report. 45:76-7. D. 5, '58. If we stand up to the Russians, they will back down. H. S. Truman.
    Text of article distributed by North American Newspaper Alliance, Inc.

United States Department of State Bulletin. 34:242-6. F. 13, '56. Record of Communist imperialism in East Germany; address. H. C. Hoover.

United States Department of State Bulletin. 36:605-10. Ap. 15, '57. Soviet-occupied zone of Germany: a case study in Communist control. E. L. Dulles.

United States Department of State Bulletin. 37:304-6. Ag. 19, '57. Berlin Declaration issued by four Western powers; text.

United States Department of State Bulletin. 38:615-20. Ap. 14, '58. Labor rejects communism—East Germany. E. L. Dulles.

United States Department of State Bulletin. 38:854-7. My. 26, '58. Lessons of Berlin; address. J. F. Dulles.

Vital Speeches of the Day. 23:356-9. Ap. 1, '57. Preservation of peace; address, March 6, 1957. Heinrich von Brentano.

Western World. p 13-17. F. '58. Answer to George Kennan. Raymond Aron.

*Western World. p35+. Jl. '58. Could we accept a neutralized Germany, united but outside NATO? J. B. Conant; Hugh Gaitskell.

World Politics. 10:366-77. Ap. '58. Reunification of Germany and security for Europe. Fritz Erler.

World Today. 12:4-7. Ja. '56. Berlin and the Soviet recognition of East German sovereignty.

1 7 6 1 9